United States
Department
of Agriculture

Forest Service

**Rocky Mountain
Research Station**

General Technical
Report RMRS-GTR-47

April 2000

Monitoring the Vegetation Resources in Riparian Areas

Alma H. Winward

I0435039

Abstract

Winward, Alma H. 2000. **Monitoring the vegetation resources in riparian areas**. Gen. Tech. Rep. RMRS-GTR-47. Ogden, UT: U.S. Department of Agriculture, Forest Service, Rocky Mountain Research Station. 49 p.

This document provides information on three sampling methods used to inventory and monitor the vegetation resources in riparian areas. The vegetation cross-section method evaluates the health of vegetation across the valley floor. The greenline method provides a measurement of the streamside vegetation. The woody species regeneration method measures the density and age class structure of any shrub or tree species that may be present in the sampling area. Together these three sampling procedures can provide an evaluation of the health of all the vegetation in a given riparian area.

Keywords: riparian sampling, vegetation cross-section, greenline, woody regeneration

The Author

Alma H. Winward is Regional Ecologist for the Intermountain Region, Forest Service in Ogden, UT. He received his B.S. degree in Range Science from Utah State University and his Ph.D. degree in Forestry Sciences from the University of Idaho. He has been involved in the ecology and management of riparian ecosystems since 1976.

Acknowledgments

Funding for this publication was provided by: Harv Forsgren, Director of Wildlife, Fish, and Rare Plants, Arthur Bryant, Director of Watershed and Air Management, Russ LaFayette, Riparian Area and Wetlands Coordinator, and Bertha Gillam, Director of Range Management, each from the Washington Office, U.S. Department of Agriculture, Forest Service; Roland M. Stoleson, Director of Vegetation Management in the Intermountain Region Office, Forest Service, Ogden, UT, and Wayne Elmore, National Riparian Service Team Leader, U.S. Department of the Interior, Bureau of Land Mangement, Prineville, OR.

The author wishes to thank Van C. Elsbernd, Rangeland Specialist, Range Management, Washington Office, Fort Collins, CO, for his support and time in assisting with all aspects in preparing this report for publication.

Special thanks are also extended to Sherel Goodrich, Warren Clary, Irwin Cowley, Sandy Wyman, Clint Williams, Curt Johnson, and Larry Bryant for their review and constructive suggestions, and to Jeanne Zschaechner for the graphics used in the document.

Rocky Mountain Research Station
324 25th Street
Ogden, UT 84401

Contents

Figures (abbreviated captions)

Tables

Monitoring the Vegetation Resources in Riparian Areas

Alma H. Winward

Introduction

Until the mid 1970's only minimal effort had been directed at monitoring the vegetation resources in riparian areas. Since that time considerable attention and research have been directed toward gaining a better understanding of the vegetation on these areas. This increased attention has been due mainly to recognition of the important sociological and economic values these areas provide to society in general.

This paper provides additional information on vegetation sampling methods first described in Winward and Pagett (1989). Subsequent publications that expanded on this initial work include USDA (1992), Cagney (1993), and several others not specifically cited. Procedures and methodologies are written to be as scientific as possible, while designed to be efficient in both time and cost. Some values used in specific ratings are based on available research and, where this is lacking, are supplemented by the professional judgment and experience of the author and various coworkers.

These procedures are specifically intended to be used as follow-up methods to the Riparian Proper Functioning (PFC) Assessment when more quantitative information is desired (USDA 1998).

The three sampling methods described in this document include: (1) Vegetation Cross Section Composition, (2) Greenline Composition, and (3) Woody Species Regeneration. The first two require that some sort of vegetation (community type) classification be available to perform the measurements. The latter method, Woody Species Regeneration, has been designed to provide information on the relative amounts of each age class of woody species found in the sampling area. All three sampling methods require a working knowledge of most of the plant species on the area being sampled.

Terminology

Colonizers—Plant species that become established in open, barren areas are among the first plants to occupy open sites. In riparian areas they colonize edges of bars or areas where streambanks have freshly eroded. They are rhizomatous/stoloniferous in growth form, but the roots are shallow and the stems are relatively weak. Although they are short lived, they have a capacity to grow very rapidly, up to 1 to 4 centimeters per day. They initiate shallow roots every few centimeters and, as water forces align their stems parallel to the water's edge, they develop temporary bands or stringers of vegetation along stream edges. Their primary function is to filter and catch

USDA Forest Service Gen. Tech. Rep. RMRS-GTR-47. 2000

1

very fine, flour-like sediments and build substrate for the stronger more permanent stabilizing species (see definition for stabilizers). As such they play a crucial role in initiating recovery and maintenance of streambanks. Typical examples include: brookgrass (*Catabrosia aquatica*) and water cress (*Rorippa nasturtium-aquaticum*) (fig. 1).

Figure 1—A typical colonizing species (brookgrass— *Catabrosia aquatica*) forming a temporary filtering community type along the greenline.

2

USDA Forest Service Gen. Tech. Rep. RMRS-GTR-47. 2000

Community type—A repeating classified and recognizable assemblage or grouping of plant species. Riparian community types represent the existing structure and composition of plant communities with no indication of successional status. They often occur as patches, stringers, or islands, and are distinguished by floristic similarities in both their overstory and understory layers.

Composition—The relative amount (percent) of one plant species or one community type in relation to other species or community types in a given area.

Greenline—The first perennial vegetation that forms a lineal grouping of community types on or near the water's edge. Most often it occurs at or slightly below the bankful stage.

Hydrophyte—A plant species found growing in areas where soils in the rooting zone are saturated much or all of the growing season.

Potential Natural Community (PNC)—The biotic community that would become established if all successional sequences were completed without human interference, under the present environmental conditions.

Riparian Complex—A unit of land with a unique set of biotic and abiotic factors. Complexes are identified on the basis of their overall geomorphology, substrate characteristics, stream gradient and associated water flow features, and general vegetation patterns. They are named after the most common or prominent community type present, along with special identifying features of the sites on which they occur, for example, Booth willow (*Salix boothii*)/Nebraska sedge (*Carex nebrascensis*)—Cryaquoll—Trough Floodplain Riparian Complex. A riparian complex is similar in definition to a valley segment, except that the valley segment refers to the stream channel proper and, thus, is normally a lineal feature (Maxwell and others 1995). The riparian complex is used to describe the full width of the riparian area across a particular portion of a valley. Generally, a limited set of stream reaches is nested within a given riparian complex.

Stabilizers—Plant species that become established along edges of streams, rivers, ponds, and lakes. Although they generally require hydric settings for establishment, some may persist in drier conditions once they have become firmly established. They commonly have strong, cord-like rhizomes as well as deep fibrous root masses. Additionally, they have coarse leaves and strong crowns, which, along with their massive root systems, are able to buffer streambanks against the erosive forces of moving water (fig. 2). Along with enhancing streambank strength, they filter sediments and, with the forces of water, they build/rebuild eroded portions of streambanks (fig. 3). They likewise filter chemicals, which is important in improving water quality. These species play a significant role in attaining and maintaining proper functioning of riparian and aquatic ecosystems.

Each stream or river must develop and maintain adequate amounts and kinds of these species or, in some cases, anchored logs or rocks, to provide, over time, a balance between the eroding and rebuilding forces of water. In this publication the terms stabilizers and hydrophytic species are essentially synonymous.

Examples include: Nebraska sedge (*Carex nebrascensis*) and Geyer's willow (*Salix geyeri*). A combination of stabilizing overstory and understory species provides the highest amount of protection possible from a vegetation standpoint. However, on low gradient systems, or on streams with low water forces, either a suitable overstory or understory component is often sufficient.

USDA Forest Service Gen. Tech. Rep. RMRS-GTR-47. 2000

3

Figure 2 — A portion of Nebraska sedge (*Carex nebrascensis*), an important stabilizing greenline species. Note its extensive, strong roots, crown, and leaves.

Figure 3 — A stream in process of recovering from a previous erosional event. Note the presence of brookgrass colonizing and collecting sediments along the water's edge. Also, note the presence of the stabilizing species Nebraska sedge forming a strong buffering line behind the brookgrass. This sequence of establishment is often one of the ways a stream channel becomes narrower after an erosional event.

Successional Status—The present state of vegetation on an area in relation to the potential natural community(ies) that could occur on that area.

Special Features

One of the more perplexing difficulties encountered when monitoring in riparian areas is the relatively small size and mosaic pattern of the community types. Individual stands of a community type may range from a few square feet in size to several acres. Any one section of a stream or meadow is usually composed of numerous, repeating stands of six to 12 community types; their pattern or distribution is tied to the soils or, most often, the water table features within that particular complex.

Another difficulty in monitoring riparian areas involves the many types of land management activities that can potentially influence the resources on these areas. Unlike surrounding upland areas, most damaging influences are not limited to the areas where they occur. Many influences become cumulative downstream or lower in the watershed. Also, some disturbance events, such as downcutting of the channel and the subsequent loss of the water table, may alter composition of the vegetation considerable distances from the down cut, usually upstream. These influences often make it difficult to understand or assign cause to particular disturbances.

Successional Processes

Vegetation monitoring generally involves selection of a representative site on which to initiate a sampling process. On upland areas, site characteristics, such as overall climate and general landscape and soil features, normally remain relatively stable over time. One can select an appropriate monitoring site and be relatively confident that most changes in the vegetation on that area, over time, can be related to whatever management is being applied.

However, in riparian areas there often is a continual process of change. Lakes and ponds gradually fill with sediments, and rivers and stream channels move about within the valley floor. These changes alone can result in an almost continual readjustment in successional processes in many areas. Even under "natural conditions," stable plant communities such as those found on upland settings can be short lived. Long term, self-perpetuating plant communities on a specific area are achieved only on a few specially armored settings where bedrock or large cobbles or boulders keep the stream channel intact or where low-gradient meadows have stable enough environments for the community types to reach a long-term balance with their environment.

This history of rapid change has produced some interesting riparian species adaptations. Many of the cottonwood, alder, birch, and willow species require, or at least regenerate much better on, disturbed or open ground. Seedlings of these species often are very poor competitors in dense grass or heavily sodded settings (Winward 1986). Instead, they depend on newly developed sand and gravel bars, freshly broken banks, or seasonal deposition areas to regenerate and establish. Similarly, many grass and sedge species establish in new sections of a stream by anchoring chunks of sod broken from banks upstream or collecting and anchoring floating seeds in openings along the stream edge. All these processes indicate a history of continual disturbances in riparian settings.

The continual disruption of succession in riparian areas does not necessarily prevent us from developing monitoring procedures based on potential of a site, nor does it leave us without an ability to use vegetation communities, in our case the community types, as descriptors of condition of an area. It means, instead, that we must accept that we are generally working with communities that often are not long-term end points in succession as we have tended to evaluate against on upland areas.

A common characteristic of the vegetation units within riparian complexes involves a gradual movement or swapping of stands of community types. As stream channels move about within a given complex or when a meander breaks and forms a stream channel in a new area of the complex, plant community types gradually develop to fit the newly created environments associated with movement of the stream and its intertied soil and water features. For example, stands of one community type can establish and exist for several years in specific locations within the complexes (figs. 4a and 4b). Then as the particular environment supporting them is altered, such as a ground water change due to a movement of the stream channel (fig. 4c), stands of that particular community type may move with the stream channel or they may reoccur somewhere else in the complex where site features become suitable (figs. 4d and 4e).

Other types suited to the newly developed settings on the original area also begin to develop. Normally, all types were present in that particular complex. Over time, stands of these types have merely "drifted" to new locations or switched places. This realignment of stands of community types is different from upland settings where stands may occur only on specific portions of a geographic area and are essentially permanent. A sampling process should be used that considers movement of site features, and subsequently, stands of the community types, as one attempts to monitor changes over time.

Riparian complexes develop and function as a result of the relatively stable interacting features of valley bottom gradient and substrate characteristics, valley bottom width, general elevation, and the size and pattern of the water forces, which are influenced by the general climate of the area. Seldom do human-related influences change these factors. Instead, human-caused influences normally involve changes in specific water table features or damaging impacts on certain plant species. These influences normally show up in changes in the community type composition within a complex.

If there is a set kind and composition of community types within a complex in undisturbed conditions, and if new types develop within that complex when unnatural disturbance factors are present, such as livestock grazing and trampling or damages from recreational or other land disturbing activities (fig. 4f), changes in kinds and amounts of community types can be measured to determine the degree of impact.

For example, new communities that may increase or develop as a result of excessive disturbances often include Kentucky bluegrass (*Poa pratensis*) and redtop (*Agrostis stolonifera*). The composition of these types in a complex can be measured and used as indicators of impact.

Additionally, if the same or a very similar riparian complex occurs in two or more different locations, we can predict potential compositions from one geographic location to another. This should allow us to understand general capabilities among similar settings and develop appropriate desired conditions and management prescriptions for similar riparian areas.

USDA Forest Service Gen. Tech. Rep. RMRS-GTR-47. 2000

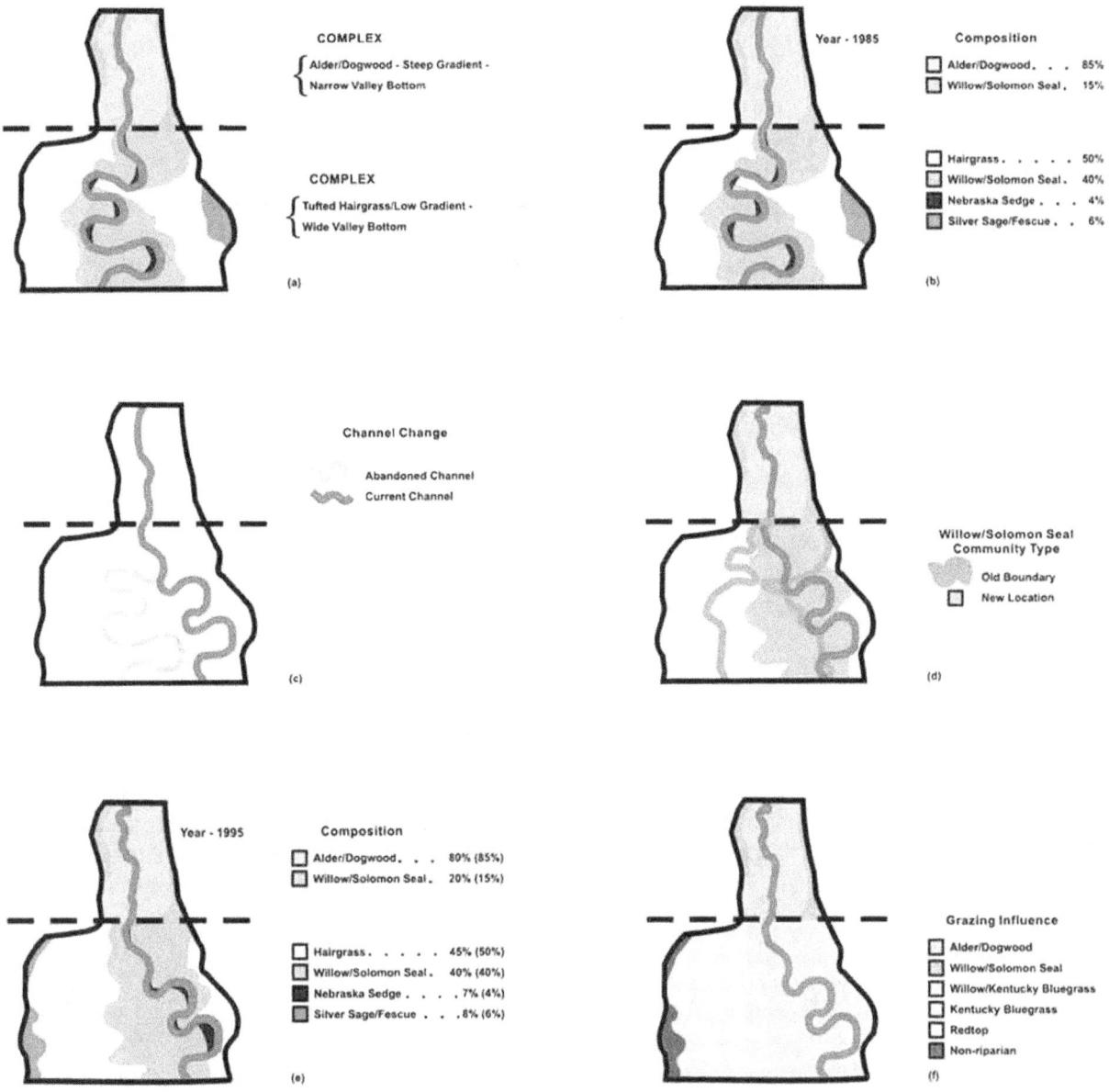

Figure 4—Graphic display of a typical riparian area: (a) two riparian complexes along with stands of several community types within each complex; (b) community type composition in two riparian complexes during sampling period 1985; (c) a stream channel change that potentially may influence location of stands of the community types; (d) realignment of stands of each community type as a result of the channel change; (e) composition changes due to channel changes, sampling period 1995; (f) common changes in kinds of community types in two complexes as a result of unnatural disturbance factors such as intensive grazing (see text discussion).

Sampling Procedures

The following sampling procedures may be used to help monitor vegetation changes taking place in riparian settings as a result of natural and human-related activities:

- Vegetation cross-section composition
- Greenline composition
- Woody species regeneration

USDA Forest Service Gen. Tech. Rep. RMRS-GTR-47. 2000

7

The line intercept method, similar to that designed for use in obtaining individual species cover (Canfield 1941), is used for obtaining community type cover and composition in procedures one and two above. Density counts of woody species by specified age classes, or in specific cases, patch sizes, are used in procedure number three.

Other common methods such as density, cover, and frequency measurements, as found in USDA (1993), may also be used where detailed evaluations are necessary. However, if these latter methods are used, one must use caution in accounting for vegetation changes caused by naturally occurring site changes compared to changes due to specific management activities (see discussion under Successional Processes, page 5).

A list of equipment needed to implement the three vegetation procedures described in this document is found in Appendix D, page 41, and forms for each procedure are found in Appendix E, pages 42-49.

Vegetation Cross-Section Composition

Each riparian complex is usually composed of a mix of stands of six to 12 community types. This procedure is designed to quantify the percent of each community type in a particular complex. These data may be used to indicate how much change has occurred in a particular complex (percent of acreage supporting altered community types), or how closely the composition of types in that area represents a previously described desired condition. Composition of types such as Kentucky bluegrass or redtop, which represent disturbance situations, can provide a measure of the percent of the complex that has been altered. Or, sampling data from similar unmodified or minimally modified riparian settings can be used as a standard to measure degree of change that may have occurred (successional status). Either of these values may then be used to compare how well an area is being managed, based on the pre-set desired conditions. Subsequent measurements in the same complex will provide information on the long-term trend of vegetation communities in that complex.

Several step transects (at least five) are established perpendicular to the grade in a riparian complex in such a way as to cross the entire riparian area (fig. 5). Each of these transects should be randomly placed in such a way as to best represent the entire complex. An aerial photograph often helps. Pacing transects has been found to be as reliable as using a measuring tape when calculating community type composition.

The beginning and ending points for each transect are permanently marked with stakes. These stakes should be placed far enough back into the non-riparian area (usually several feet) to allow subsequent quantification in case the riparian area expands in size. Placement there also helps ensure that stakes are not damaged or lost during an unusually high flooding event.

Community type composition is obtained by taking the number of steps encountered for each type in all five transects divided by the total number of steps taken in all five transects.

$$\frac{\text{Number of steps in each community type}}{\text{Total number of steps}} = \frac{\text{Community type}}{\text{Composition}}$$

USDA Forest Service Gen. Tech. Rep. RMRS-GTR-47. 2000

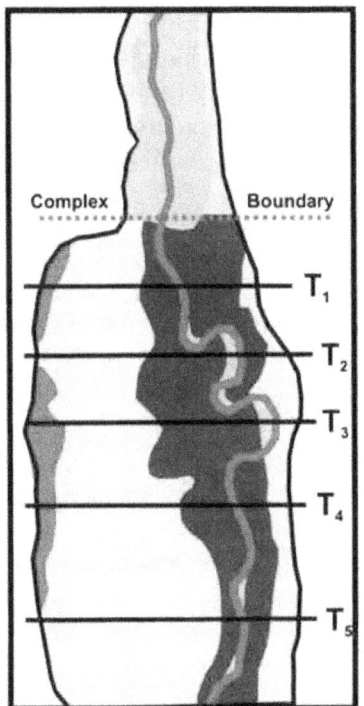

Community Type

☐ Alder/dogwood
☐ Willow/solomon seal
■ Willow/beaked sedge
☐ Kentucky bluegrass
☐ Beaked sedge
▨ Redtop

Figure 5— Vegetation cross-section measurement. Use of the line intercept method to measure amount of change in community type composition within a complex after unnatural disturbances.

Example:

Community type	T1	T2	T3	T4	T5		Steps (ct)		Steps total		Percent comp
Willow/beaked sedge	40	45	40	35	20	=	180	/	480	=	38
Kentucky bluegrass	50	50	45	45	75	=	265	/	480	=	55
Beaked sedge	0	5	10	0	0	=	15	/	480	=	3
Redtop	5	0	10	5	0	=	20	/	480	=	4
					Total	=	480				100

Since the Kentucky bluegrass community type (55 percent) and the redtop community type (4 percent) represent disturbance types in this complex, 59 percent of the area (55 + 4) has altered types present. Specific procedures for evaluating cross-sectional data are shown in the Data Analysis Procedures (page 22).

Since the number of steps in each community type is ultimately calculated to percent composition, average length of each step does not need to be measured as long as one person performs all pacing on any given transect and the overall width of the riparian-wetland area is not needed. (Generally, aerial extent of the riparian area can be more accurately obtained using GIS technology.)

A hand-held tally counter will aid in using this sampling process.

Any community type fragment encountered that is less than one step in length will normally not be tallied separately. Instead that fragment will be tallied with the most common adjacent type.

USDA Forest Service Gen. Tech. Rep. RMRS-GTR-47. 2000

9

Photographs should be taken, as a minimum, at each of the permanent cross-section stakes and should display the general setting of the transect. Photographs may also be taken where the transect crosses the stream channel or at other locations along the transect where a pictorial record will be useful in visualizing specific features of the area.

Greenline Composition

Sampling community type composition along the greenline (see definition, page 3) can provide additional information over that collected by the cross-section process. Presence of more or less permanent water in the plant-rooting zone allows growth of robust, hydrophytic plant species that play an important role in buffering the forces of water. Additionally, vegetation in these favorable environments can often recover rapidly after either natural or induced disturbances. This permits the land manager to make an early evaluation of effects of management on a particular area. If subsequent measurements are made in the same area 3 to 5 years apart, data can be compared to provide indications of long-term trend for that riparian area.

Also, there is a strong interrelationship between amount and kind of vegetation along the water's edge and bank stability (Dunaway and others 1994; Kleinfelder and others 1992; Manning and others 1989; Weixelman and others 1996). The majority of naturally occurring plant species in this more or less permanently watered area have rooting characteristics (including strength, length, and mass) that enhance bank stability.

Evaluation of the vegetation on the greenline area provides a good indication of a streambank's ability to buffer the hydrologic forces of moving water. And, since the greenline is located where the forces of water are greatest, a greenline measurement can provide an indication of health of the total watershed above the point of sampling.

Locating and Measuring the Greenline—In most riparian settings, there is a continual natural process in place to develop a buffering line of protective vegetation on each side of the stream. At the same time, there is continual cutting action by water forces to erode away this vegetation. Each stream or river must develop adequate amounts and kinds of plant species to maintain, over time, a balance between the eroding and rebuilding forces of water. Specific amounts depend on the erosive features of the riparian complex involved, particularly stream gradient and substrate materials. Those with the greatest water forces and weaker substrate materials will naturally have a higher percentage of the greenline made up of colonizing or early successional plant species compared to stabilizing hydrophytic species. Generally, not every foot of bank will be totally protected by a continuous coverage of robust, hydrophytic species. In some riparian complexes, large boulders, bedrock, or occasionally anchored logs or debris play a similar role in reducing bank erosion. Based on the hydrologic features of each riparian complex, there must be sufficient bank protection to maintain function of that stream type (see estimated values presented as needed or required for various groupings of riparian complexes in Appendix A, page 34).

Most often the greenline is located at or near the bankful stage (fig. 6). As flows recede and the vegetation continues to develop summer growth, it may be located part way out on a gravel or sandbar (fig. 7). At times when banks are freshly eroding or, especially when a stream has become entrenched, the greenline may be located several feet above bank-full stage (fig. 8). In these

Figure 6—Location of the greenline at or near the bank-full stage.

Figure 7—Location of the greenline after summer water flows have decreased.

USDA Forest Service Gen. Tech. Rep. RMRS-GTR-47. 2000

11

Figure 8—Location of the greenline on an eroded bank. Following the definition of greenline, "the first line of perennial vegetation that forms a lineal grouping of community types on or near the waters edge," the eroded non-riparian portion of the streambank serves as the current greenline (see further discussion on location of the greenline in fig. 9).

situations, the vegetation is seldom represented by hydrophytic species and, in fact, may be composed of non-riparian species (fig. 9).

Greenline Sampling—The greenline measurement is designed to account for a continuous line of vegetation on each side of the stream even when this line of vegetation occurs several feet above or away from the stream's edge. The only (rare) exception to this continuous line is where a road or trail crosses the stream or where a sidestream enters the stream being measured. In these cases, the width, in steps, should be tallied as road/trail or stream and included in the tally of early successional representation (discussed later). It is important that the greenline sampling process follow these continuous lines of vegetation rather than the seasonally fluctuating water's edge. This helps ensure that measurements are made on the best representative area for evaluating changes in vegetation over more than one sampling period.

Disturbance activities, such as overgrazing or trampling by animals or people, result in vegetation changes to shallower, weakly rooted species such as Kentucky bluegrass or redtop (fig. 10). These species have a reduced ability to buffer the forces of moving water and keep the stream's hydrologic features in balance. Therefore, an evaluation of the vegetation composition on the greenline can provide a valuable indication of the general health of a

Figure 9—Example of greenline supporting non-riparian vegetation. As areas such as this begin to heal, the angle of the bank will become less steep and a greenline composed primarily of hydrophytic vegetation will begin to form near the water's edge. Over a period of time the sinuosity of the stream channel will adjust to fit the hydrologic features of the site in concert with the appropriate amounts and kinds of greenline vegetation. Until this occurs, non-riparian community types may serve as the measured greenline edge.

Figure 10—Example of a greenline dominated by non-hydrophytic plant species. Note the excessive streambank erosion on portions of this bank due to dominance of shallow-rooted species.

riparian area (successional status) as well as the current strength of the streambanks in buffering the forces of water (streambank stability).

The greenline sampling procedure requires that a vegetation community type classification be completed for the area being measured (fig. 11). Since plant species on an area generally act together as groups, an evaluation based on community type composition provides a better measurement of health and strength of the vegetation components on an area than a more complicated process where individual plants are measured and evaluated separately.

The greenline sampling measurement should be taken within one riparian complex (fig. 12). Depending on length of the complex, one or more samples may be necessary to provide adequate representation of that complex. To minimize efforts and dollars, sampling placement should emphasize measurements in the complex, or complexes, most subject to influences by the particular disturbance factors in that drainage.

General location of the transect(s) within the complex should be selected to best represent influences of major activities in that complex and should be agreed on by individuals from all disciplines interested in management of the area. Often an aerial photo can be helpful in selecting the sampling location(s). In settings where a stream has multiple channels, the current, most active channel should be followed.

The starting point for the transect may be randomly selected within the complex or it may be located where a cross-section transect intercepts the stream (fig. 13). If both greenline and cross-section measurements are taken in the same general area, a more complete evaluation of the streamside and valley bottom health within a given complex will be possible.

A greenline transect begins on the right-hand side looking downstream and proceeds down the greenline using a step transect approach as described in

Figure 11 — Stands of several community types in the riparian complex.

Figure 12—Example of two riparian complexes: Complex A—Narrowleaf cottonwood/Kentucky bluegrass, Haploboroll, moderate gradient, narrow valley bottom, and Complex B—Coyote willow/Kentucky bluegrass, Cryaquoll, low gradient, broad valley bottom riparian complexes.

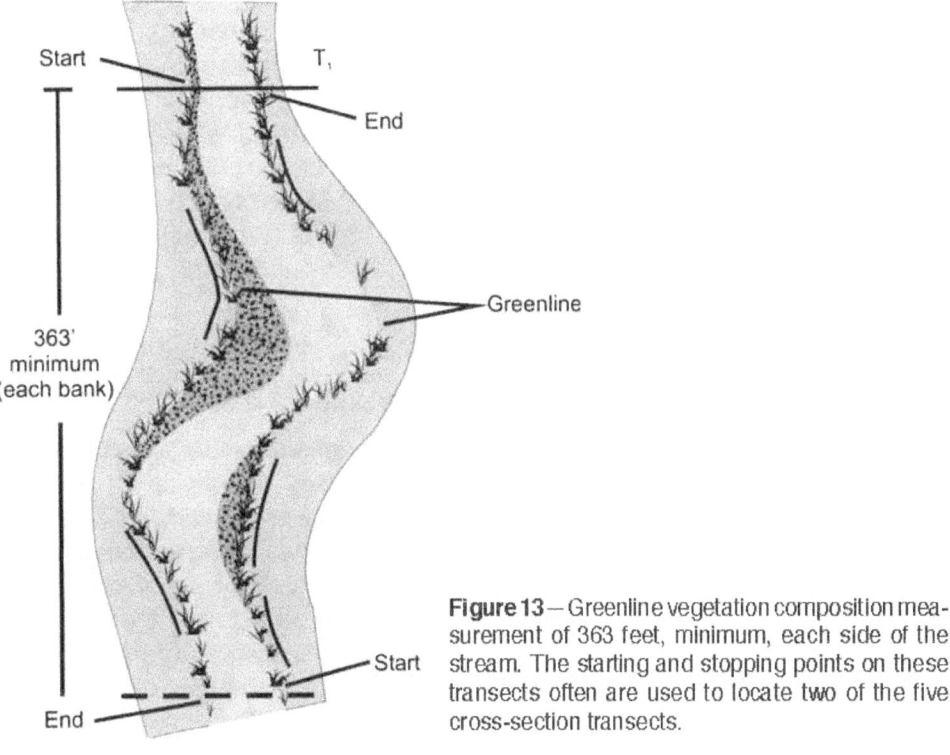

Figure 13—Greenline vegetation composition measurement of 363 feet, minimum, each side of the stream. The starting and stopping points on these transects often are used to locate two of the five cross-section transects.

USDA Forest Service Gen. Tech. Rep. RMRS-GTR-47. 2000

15

the cross-section measurement. For each greenline measurement, enough steps should be taken to total a minimum of 363 feet lineal distance on each side of the stream. This minimum distance (363 feet each side) will help ensure that the sampler measures an adequate length of stream to encompass the potential variation within a riparian complex. Additionally, this length is important when conducting data collection of woody species regeneration (described later). A temporary marker is placed at the end of the transect for location of the follow-up measurement of woody species regeneration. The beginning and ending points of these transects may be permanently marked with stakes to provide for greater repeatability for future and different workers. However, because of the transient movement of stream channels, it is recommended that these points be tied to a nearby reference point, away from stream edges, so that subsequent sampling will be done as near to the initial sampling area as is feasible. The overall goal is to get a reliable measurement of streamside vegetation in that complex.

The sampler then crosses the stream and repeats the sampling process for 363 feet upstream. It is important to measure both sides of the stream since grazing pressures or water forces may be different on each side. (NOTE: The stopping point may not coincide with the initial starting point on the other side of the stream due to differences in lengths of meanders on each side of the stream. Divide the average length of the person's step doing the sampling into 363 feet to determine minimum number of steps to take on each side of the stream, for example, 363 feet divided by 2.5 ft/step = 145 steps each side).

On certain streams, especially those with steeper gradients, large rocks and downed logs may serve, along with the vegetation, to buffer water forces on the greenline. The number of feet of large anchored rocks or logs encountered on the greenline edge should be tallied in place of the vegetation. These rocks and logs must be large enough to withstand the forces of water and must appear stable in the setting. The number of feet of these rocks and logs will be counted as a natural, stable percentage of the greenline.

The greenline measurement becomes less valuable in monitoring steeper (greater than 4 percent gradient) streams since the large, permanently anchored rocks are generally less susceptible to management activities. Also, the greenline measurement may be a less valuable measurement on very large rivers where landform features play the dominant role in regulating hydrologic influences compared to vegetation influences.

The total number of steps of each community type encountered along the greenline on both sides of the stream is tallied and percent composition for each type computed, as described in the cross-section composition measurement. For example:

$$\frac{\text{Total steps of each type (both sides)}}{\text{Total steps taken both sides}} = \frac{\text{Percent community type}}{\text{Composition}}$$

If one is interested in evaluating whether one side of the stream has been impacted more than the other side, divide the community type values on each side by the number of steps for each side and compare values.

An evaluation of percent of disturbance types in relation to percent of natural types (see cross-section computation) provides a general indication of ecological status. If available, a comparison of areas where the complex is as close to potential natural community (PNC) as possible may be used as a standard or reference to evaluate successional status of the area being measured. Subsequent measurements of the same area will provide a measurement of trend for that complex. See the Data Analyses Procedures section to find descriptions of all methods for analyzing greenline data (page 22).

A photograph should be taken at the starting and ending points of the greenline transect. Additional photos may be taken along the transect if desired. These photographs should contain relatively permanent reference points or markers (such as boulders or large trees) so the photographs can be re-established in the future.

Woody Species Regeneration

A measurement of woody species regeneration is made using a 6-foot wide belt along the same transects used for the greenline measurements (figs. 14 and 15).

The sampler uses a 6-foot pole that has the center marked. Measurements are made by walking a minimum of 363 feet on each side of the stream (726 total feet), with the marked center of the pole held directly over the inside edge of the greenline.

Use of the greenline edge as the center of the measurement helps to ensure that sampling is done in a setting where regeneration of woody species is most likely to occur. The distances indicated will result in sampling 0.1 acre (726 x 6 = 4,356 sq ft), which is normally considered an adequate sample area for this type of measurement. NOTE: Where the greenline edge is immediately adjacent to the stream edge, 3 feet of the pole will extend over water (fig. 16).

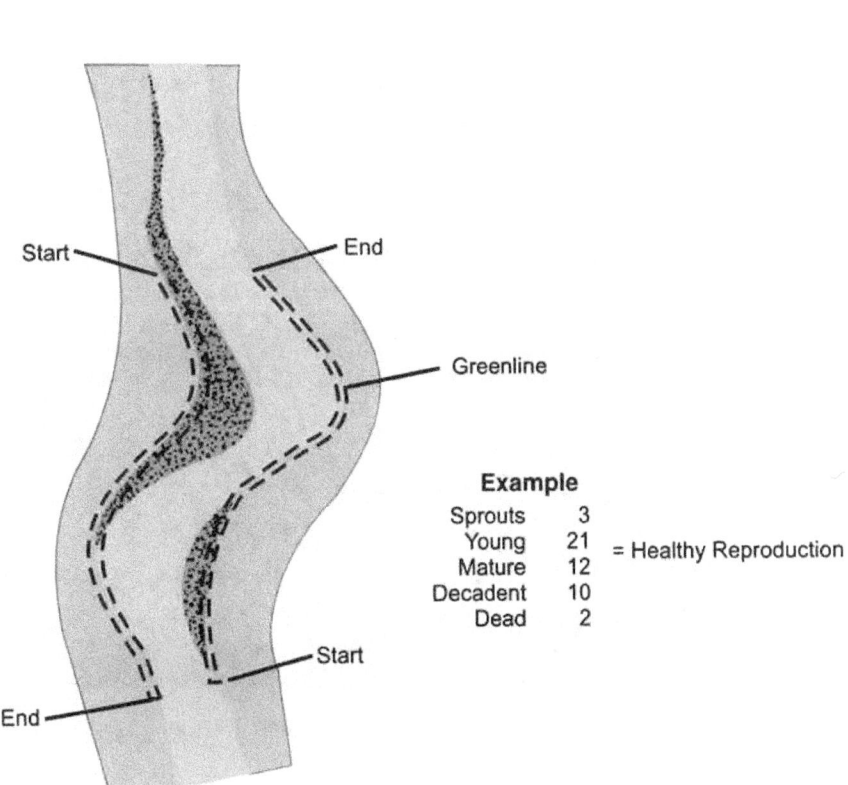

Figure 14—Woody species counts by age class.

USDA Forest Service Gen. Tech. Rep. RMRS-GTR-47. 2000

17

Figure 15—Samplers using a 6-foot pole to measure woody species regeneration along the greenline.

Figure 16—Correct placement of the sampling pole along the greenline water interface.

But, where a recently developed gravel or sand bar is present (see fig. 7, page 11), this measurement will allow sampling on the most likely place where most woody species regenerate, the open bars. Additionally, using this approach will result in consistently sampling 0.1 acre.

A modification of this procedure will be necessary for situations where the stream is less than 3 feet across. Where this occurs, the measurer should not allow the left tip of the pole to extend beyond the center of the stream, as this would result in double sampling of the middle portion of the stream when the other side is measured (fig. 17).

All, or selected, woody plants rooted within the ends of the pole are tallied based on the following age-class categories.

Clumped, multiple-stemmed species (most willows):

Number of stems at ground surface	Age class
1	Sprout
2 to 10	Young
>10, >$^1/_2$ stems alive	Mature
>10, <$^1/_2$ stems alive	Decadent
0 stems alive	Dead

Rhizomatous species (patches):

For rhizomatous willow species that form more or less continuous patches, such as wolf willow (*Salix wolfii*), planeleaf willow (*S. planifolia*), or wild rose (*Rosa* spp.), use permanently marked line transect measurements to follow changes in patch sizes over time. Use both greenline and cross-section transect data or establish several permanently marked 100-foot transects randomly located within the complex (fig. 18).

Figure 17—Placement of the measuring pole such that the left end does not reach beyond the center of a stream less than 6 feet wide.

USDA Forest Service Gen. Tech. Rep. RMRS-GTR-47. 2000

19

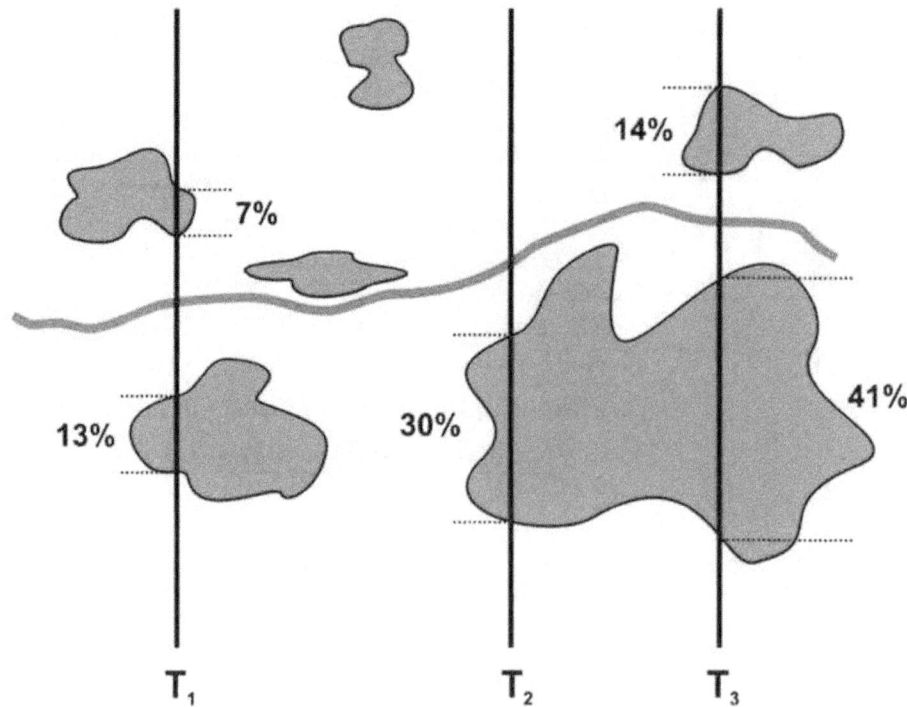

Figure 18— Use of line transect data to determine percent shrub or tree canopy for species that occur in patches. T1 = 7 + 13 = 20; T2 = 30; T3 = 14 + 41 = 55. Total = 20 + 30 + 55 = 105. (105/300 = 35% willow canopy cover).

Single-stemmed species:

For shrub and tree species that tend to grow more single stemmed, such as coyote willow (*Salix exigua*), birch (*Betula* spp.), alder (*Alnus* spp.), and cottonwoods or quaking aspen (*Populus* spp.), count each stem that occurs 12 or more inches from any other at ground level as a separate plant, and age them by pre-established categories. As a minimum, four categories—sprout, young, mature, and dead—should be developed based on a combination of both growth rings and unbrowsed height.

Example:

Growth rings*	Height	Age class
1-2	$<\frac{1}{4}$ mature	sprout
3-10	$<\frac{1}{2}$ mature	young
>10	near full	mature
—	—	dead

*Specific values vary by species.

NOTE: Stems cut or cored for developing growth ring categories should not be taken from within the 6-foot wide transect belt. Observations or measurements of the mature shrubs and trees in the general area can usually serve as references for age and height categories.

Even though there may be little or no information concerning potential densities of the shrub and tree species on an area, measurement of the age-class distribution can provide an evaluation of whether management is satisfactory to maintain or eventually reach appropriate coverages and densities of woody species capable of being present on that area. It is assumed

20

USDA Forest Service Gen. Tech. Rep. RMRS-GTR-47. 2000

that if management is such that sustained recruitment is in progress, eventually that area will support appropriate amounts of woody species needed to provide a naturally functioning complex.

Several factors can influence recruitment and death ratios of woody plants at any one location.

Recruitment:

1. Seed crop year—there is a high amount of variation in seed production between years.

2. Amount and availability of sites suitable for establishment any given year (see continuing discussion in this section).

Death:

1. Excessive drying or prolonged ponding of sites due to lowering or raising of water tables or movement of the stream channel to a new location in the valley bottom.

2. Cutting away of the root wad due to channel adjustments.

3. Occasional death from diseases.

4. Prolonged excessive browsing along with any of the above factors.

5. A combination of beaver cutting along with any of the above factors.

Not all riparian areas are well suited for growing woody species. This is especially true where the complex has a low gradient and a limited amount of natural stream channel movement, and on anaerobic meadow soils that are often saturated to or near the surface during the growing season. In these settings, understory sedges and rushes often are able to buffer the forces of water without the addition of woody species. Most woody riparian species regenerate best on settings where there are aerobic soil conditions and, at least temporarily, minimal competition from herbaceous species. Generally speaking, if the stream being monitored has a gradient over 0.5 percent or has water forces adequate to periodically cut banks and deposit bars, it is capable of supporting a woody overstory of willows, alder, birch, or cottonwood. On streams with gradients of less than 0.5 percent, streambanks generally can be adequately protected by robust sedges, rushes, and grasses. Woody species are seldom naturally present on the greenline in these settings.

The amount and continuity of stream riffles, as tied to gradient, may be used to broadly identify streams with water forces adequate to provide habitat for woody species. A stream can support a considerable coverage of shrubs and trees if it has a more or less continuous presence of riffles. An exception to this is small spring-fed systems where gradients are sufficient to provide riffles in the stream, but the relatively stable water forces are not adequate to cut streambanks and deposit bars. In these settings robust herbaceous species are adequate to protect the streambanks and maintain hydrologic processes; a shrubby component will not likely be present.

A stream that has intermittent riffles with long pools of dead water generally supports islands or patches of woody vegetation in the complex. Once established, these patches may persist for many years, even as the stream, over time, meanders to new locations in that complex.

An accurate evaluation of the cover or density of shrubs and trees that should be present on an area cannot be known or approximated without having data from a similar complex that is in a somewhat natural condition. In absence of this information, a measurement of age-class distribution of woody species can indicate whether current management is allowing an

USDA Forest Service Gen. Tech. Rep. RMRS-GTR-47. 2000

21

adequate amount of recruitment to sustain or recover the woody component in a particular complex. Generally, there should be several times more plants present in the sprout and young categories as in the mature and dead categories. This is especially true if an area has recently begun recovery of the woody component. Complexes where the sprouts and young age classes are less than the mature and dead classes will not likely sustain a shrub and tree component over the long term.

Even though the current shoots on multi-stemmed species, such as willows, resprout every 10 to 20 years, the crown portion of these plants may remain alive for over 100 years—as long as the habitat features, especially water tables, remain in place.

Where the willow component has been completely lost from an area, mounded areas that develop under long-term presence of shrub crowns may provide evidence that willows or other woody species were once present in a particular complex. These remnant mounds, or in some cases remnant stems or crowns, may persist for several decades after the plants have been lost from an area.

Recent studies have shown that it is extremely difficult and time consuming to accurately measure utilization (browsing) impacts on many riparian shrubs (Hall 1999). Until more acceptable methodologies are developed, it is suggested that only a general estimate on overall browsing on the woody plants be recorded in the comments section of the form. For example (USDA 1993):

Percent use	Use class
0-5	No use
6-20	Slight
21-40	Light
41-60	Moderate
61-80	Heavy
81-100	Severe

There generally is a reduction in seed production on those plants that have utilization values above 55 percent. There can be a reduction in the overall health of plants, including size and root strength, when heavy and severe utilization levels are sustained over time.

It is important that measurements or estimates be taken on the younger aged shrubs since these plants are most likely to have, and show, impacts from browsing. These young plants must have an opportunity to develop into mature plants over time. If there is sustained recruitment of shrubs and trees, an area will maintain or eventually support appropriate amounts of woody plants to provide a naturally functioning system.

Data Analysis Procedures

These procedures are in addition to the procedure described on pages 8-16, where percent of a complex that has altered types present provides an indication of impact. Use vegetation composition data from the cross-section or greenline measurements to rate status of an area in one or more of the following ways:

Successional Status—Using Coefficient of Community Type Similarity (2w/a + b)

(a) = Sum of PNC values measured in a similar complex in an unmodified condition.

(b) = Sum of values for present composition.

(w) = Sum of the values common to both.

This procedure requires use of data from a similar complex sampled in as unaltered condition as is possible (see Potential Natural Community (PNC) values, table 1).

Therefore, similarity index (2w/a + b) = (2 x 45/100 + 100) = 45 percent, or mid successional status. NOTE: When values used in "a" and "b" have been calculated to percent composition (100 percent), the successional status rating and the "w" value are the same; no calculation is necessary.

Similarity to PNC		Successional status
0-15		Very early seral
16-40		Early seral
41-60	→	Mid seral
61-85		Late seral
86+		PNC

Desired Condition—Using Coefficient of Community Type Similarity

Use where a decision has been made to manage an area for a seral stage other than PNC (2w/a + b) – table 2.

A similarity value of 75 percent or greater is often used to differentiate between meeting or not meeting management objectives.

Therefore, Area One similarity index (2w/a + b) of (2 x 78/100 + 100) = 78 percent. (Area One is 78 percent of desired condition = meeting management objectives.)

Therefore, Area Two similarity index of (2 x 19/100 + 100) = 19 percent. (Area Two is 19 percent of desired condition = not meeting management objectives.)

Table 1—Example of successional status of vegetation using Coefficient of Community Similarity (modified from Winward 1989).

Community type	Composition potential natural community	Composition present community	Amount in common
	- - - - - - - - - - - - - - - - Percent - - - - - - - - - - - - - - - - -		
Booth willow/beaked sedge	65	30	30
Water sedge	5	5	5
Beaked sedge	15	10	10
Kentucky bluegrass	0	55	0
Solomon-seal/winged sedge	15	0	0
	a = 100	b = 100	w = 45

Table 2—Examples of ratings for two different areas representing the Booth willow/beaked sedge-moderate gradient riparian type in relation to desired community type composition values (modified from Winward 1989).

Community type	Composition	Desired composition		Amount in common	
		Area One	Area Two	Area One	Area Two
		Percent			
Booth willow/beaked sedge	20	16	3	16	3
Wolfs willow/hairgrass	5	3	1	3	1
Water sedge	7	2	1	2	1
Beaked sedge	60	50	8	50	8
Baltic rush	3	10	10	3	3
Kentucky bluegrass	0	5	47	0	0
Mesic forb	3	13	30	3	3
False-hellebore	2	1	0	1	0
	a = 100	b = 100	b = 100	w = 78	w = 19

Greenline Successional Status and Bank Stability

Since there often is limited information concerning which community types indicate excessive or unnatural disturbances, and because it is extremely difficult to find examples of PNC situations in riparian areas, the following procedures may be used to broadly rate riparian areas as to their successional status and relative bank stability.

Ten capability groups (Appendix A, page 34) have been developed based on:

1. Percent stream gradient (similar to those presented in Rosgen 1996).
2. Certain substrate features that may substantially influence erosiveness of streambanks:

   (a) dominant soil particle sizes such as silts, sands, gravels, and
   (b) presence of at least one major soil horizon within the rooting zone that consists of strongly compacted, cohesive, or cemented particles (consolidated materials) (fig. 19).

Each of these 10 groups has specific, inherent environmental characteristics, which influence the amount and kind of vegetation necessary for them to function properly. An "expected value" percent of late successional community types along the greenline has been assigned to each of these groups (see values in parentheses, Appendix A). These percent values are based on the minimum amount of late successional community types that would be expected to occur when areas representing each capability group are in good health and functioning properly.

Additionally, a list has been developed of all community types known to occur on lands administered by the Intermountain Region, Forest Service (Appendix B, page 35). In this list, each community type has been assigned an "L" if it is known to occur in later successional stages along the greenline, or an "E" if known to occur in earlier stages of succession along the greenline.

Each community type also has been assigned a stability class ranking. This ranking ranges from 1, those types least capable of buffering the forces of moving water, to 10, those types with the highest buffering capabilities. The rating is based on the strength, amount, and depth of roots, as well as special leaf and crown features. As community type classifications are developed for

24

USDA Forest Service Gen. Tech. Rep. RMRS-GTR-47. 2000

Figure 19—Substrate features, in this case a consolidated soil layer, may substantially influence erosiveness of stream banks.

other areas, successional status categories (early or late) and bank stability ratings (1 to 10) will need to be developed for each of these types.

Percent composition of each community type from the greenline measurements is used to make both the successional status and bank stability ratings. The procedures are:

Greenline Successional Status Based On Capability Groups—To determine greenline successional status, use information provided in Appendix B, page 35, to arrange the community type composition values into either the Early or Late columns (see example, Greenline Successional Status, Appendix C, page 40). Summarize all types that occur in the Late column and divide by the expected value for that particular capability group (Appendix A). This will provide an intertie to the ecological potential of the area being measured. Rating of ecological status is then determined by comparing this number with those assigned to each of the five status values:

$$
\begin{array}{rcl}
0\text{-}15 & = & \text{Very early} \\
16\text{-}40 & = & \text{Early} \\
41\text{-}60 & = & \text{Mid} \\
61\text{-}85 & = & \text{Late} \\
86+ & = & \text{PNC}
\end{array}
$$

Greenline Bank Stability—The greenline stability rating is calculated by multiplying the percent composition of each community type along the greenline by the stability class rating assigned to that type (Appendix B, page 35). These index values are then summed and compared to the appropriate rating classes:

USDA Forest Service Gen. Tech. Rep. RMRS-GTR-47. 2000

25

$$
\begin{aligned}
1\text{-}2 &= \text{Very low} \\
3\text{-}4 &= \text{Low} \\
5\text{-}6 &= \text{Mid} \\
7\text{-}8 &= \text{High} \\
9\text{-}10 &= \text{Excellent}
\end{aligned}
$$

See example of Greenline Stability calculations (Appendix C, page 40).

These successional status and stability ratings may now be evaluated against standards set for the general area being studied; management can be adjusted if these standards are not being met.

Procedures for Refining the Calculation of Successional Status

Proportioning Transitional Types—Because of the many natural, or induced, disturbances that are ongoing in riparian areas, it is not uncommon to encounter community types that are in transition, developing into new or different community types. For example, as an area progressively recovers from a past disturbance, successional processes may move it from a Kentucky bluegrass community type toward a Nebraska sedge type. The community type classification keys generally handle these situations by prioritizing which plant species occur first in the keys. For example, an area supporting greater than 20 percent cover of both Nebraska sedge and Kentucky bluegrass would key to a Nebraska sedge type because Nebraska sedge occurs ahead of Kentucky bluegrass in the community type key. A pure Nebraska sedge type is higher on the successional scale than a mixed Nebraska sedge—Kentucky bluegrass type and the intertied influences on such things as bank stability are likewise considerably different.

If an area being sampled is going through a relatively rapid rate of recovery or degradation, and if one is having difficulty discerning which of two community types are being encountered in the area being sampled (near equal amounts of two different indicator species are occurring together), one should consider using the following approach:

- Determine which of the two indicator species is more prominent.

- Record the more prominent species first with the secondary indicator species immediately behind it—in parentheses.

 For example, *Juncus balticus* (*Poa pratensis*) would indicate that *Juncus* is slightly more prominent than *Poa*.

- Initially record and calculate percent composition of this blended type as one "type."

- When calculating successional status and streambank stability, count the species listed first (in this case *Juncus*) as 60 percent of the composition and the species in parentheses as 40 percent.

 For example, if the composition of this blended type = 30 percent of all types on the area, then

 30% composition x 60% = 18% of *Juncus*
 30% composition x 40% = 12% of *Poa*

The 60/40 percent values have been selected to provide a refinement in calculation of successional status and streambank stability over a process that does not recognize this relatively common blending of types. It is recommended that this proportioning procedure be used where there are relatively high composition values of more than one indicator species in the community type being evaluated. Any subsequent measurements, taken several years later, should allow one to determine which of the indicators is becoming more prominent under current management.

Examples: Assume the area is in a transitional mode of recovery; *Poa pratensis* (*Popr*) is prevalent throughout the area, but plants of *Carex nebrascensis* (*Cane*) and *Juncus balticus* (*Juba*) are increasing enough to appear near codominant with the *Poa*.

Community types	Steps	Percent composition
Popr	200 / 230 =	87%
Juba	30 / 230 =	13%
Total = 230		100%

(a) Not proportioning types

Successional status	Early	Late
Kentucky bluegrass	87	
Baltic rush		13

13% Late seral types = Very Early successional status

(b) Proportioning types

Popr (*Cane*) $\quad$ 87% x 60 = Popr = 52%
$\qquad\qquad\quad$ 87% x 40 = Cane = 35%

Juba (*popr*) $\quad$ 13% x 60 = Juba = 8%
$\qquad\qquad\quad$ 13% x 40 = Popr = 5%
$\qquad\qquad\qquad\qquad\qquad\qquad\quad$ 100%

Popr = 52 + 5 = 57% = Early
Cane = $\quad\quad\quad$ 35% = Late
Juba = $\quad\quad\quad\;$ 8% = Late
$\qquad\qquad$ 100%

35% + 8% = 43% Late seral types = Mid successional status

Proportioning of the types has indicated there is a high enough presence of the late successional species to rate the area mid, compared to very early ecological status, where types were not proportioned. Continuation of the proportioning process into the streambank stability calculations will likewise allow one to make a more sensitive evaluation of bank stability.

Adjusting the Successional Status Rating for Areas Where a Woody Overstory Component Should be Present but Currently is not Present—Calculation of successional status for riparian areas that historically supported trees or shrubs, but currently have little or no woody overstory present, may result in an over-inflated rating. For example, if an area historically supported a Booth willow/beaked sedge community type, but due to various disturbances currently only supports a beaked sedge type, the rating process described under (a) "Greenline Successional Status Based on Capability Groups," would rate both types the same. This results because both types are rated in the Late Succession category (see Appendix B). If an area historically supported the willow/sedge community, it can generally be assumed the area is adapted to function better with both the willow and sedge components present. Consequently, an ecological status rating would need to account for this difference.

Solution:

If the stream being monitored has a gradient greater than 0.5 percent and has water forces adequate to periodically cut banks and deposit bars (see discussion, page 21), it likely should support a hydrophytic woody overstory component. If it does not, as evaluated using the Woody Species Regeneration data:

Lower the calculated Ecological Status score:

- Twenty (20) points if no hydrophytic woody plants are present.

- Ten (10) points if all age classes are present but one or more of the age classes is nearly absent or obviously under-represented.

  NOTE: A healthy age class representation should include slightly more plants in the sprouts and young categories than in the mature and dead categories.

There are several important reasons to have woody species on streams that historically had them, including:

1. Protection and strengthening of streambanks (woody plant roots generally extend deeper into the soil profile and are stronger than roots of herbaceous species).
2. Structural diversity.
3. Species diversity.
4. Stream shading.
5. Habitat values tied to foraging, hiding and thermal cover, nesting sites, and others.

There is limited information to establish numerical values for all these factors. Consequently, values provided to adjust the ecological status ratings when woody species are absent, or not adequately represented, are meant to be approximations. They are given to provide more consistency for workers calculating ecological status ratings than if no values were given.

It is essential that the sampler(s) record in the comments section of the forms what adjustments were made and why.

1. When encountering an obstacle (bush or tree) while pacing the greenline or vegetation cross-section transects, sidestep the object and tally only the forward steps:

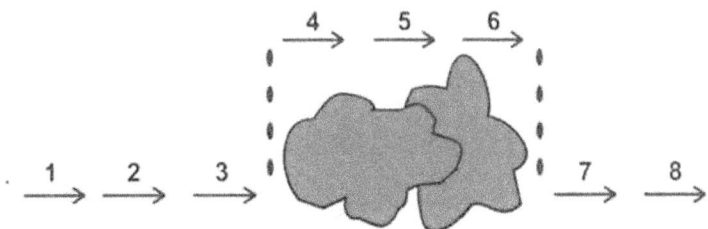

2. At times when attempting to run a cross-section transect through a very wide valley bottom, 0.25 mile or more, it becomes infeasible both in time and expense to complete a full transect. In such cases it may be appropriate to select only a portion of the valley bottom for measurement. It is recommended that one consider (1) the specific impacting factors occurring in the overall valley, and (2) what portion of the valley may be measured to best represent those impacting factors. Use permanent marking stakes to identify where transects were run. Clearly indicate in the remarks section of the form reasons for selecting that specific portion of the valley, and sketch a clear diagram of where all five transects were run.

3. Occasionally, as one is pacing a cross-section transect, it becomes difficult to identify, specifically, where certain community type boundaries occur. It often is helpful to look several feet on each side of the line that one is traversing to better select where a boundary occurs. This is especially critical where one of the community types has a relatively sparse component in the overstory, for example, willows, shrubby cinquefoil (*Potentilla fruticosa*), or silver sage (*Artemisia cana*):

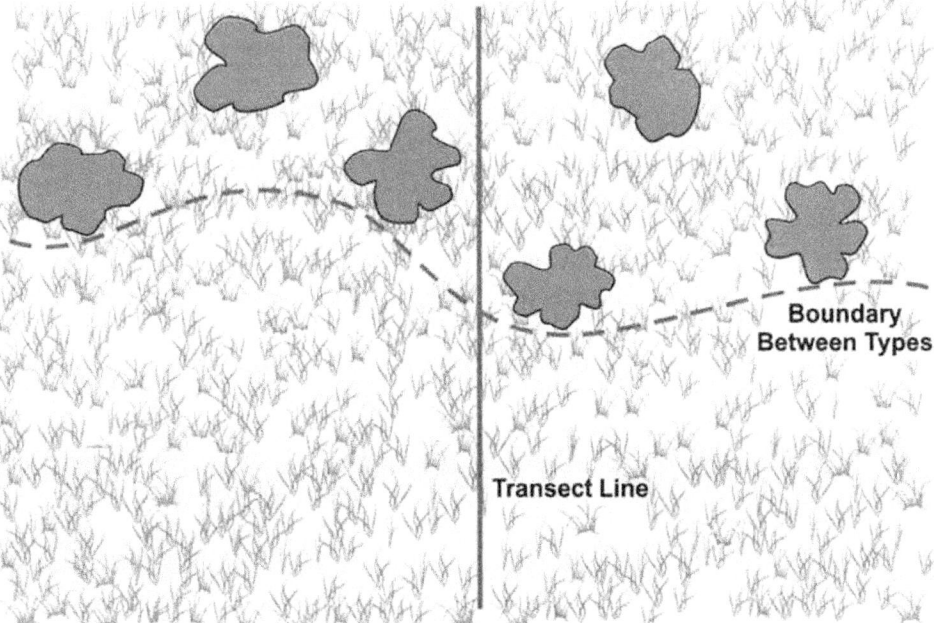

USDA Forest Service Gen. Tech. Rep. RMRS-GTR-47. 2000

29

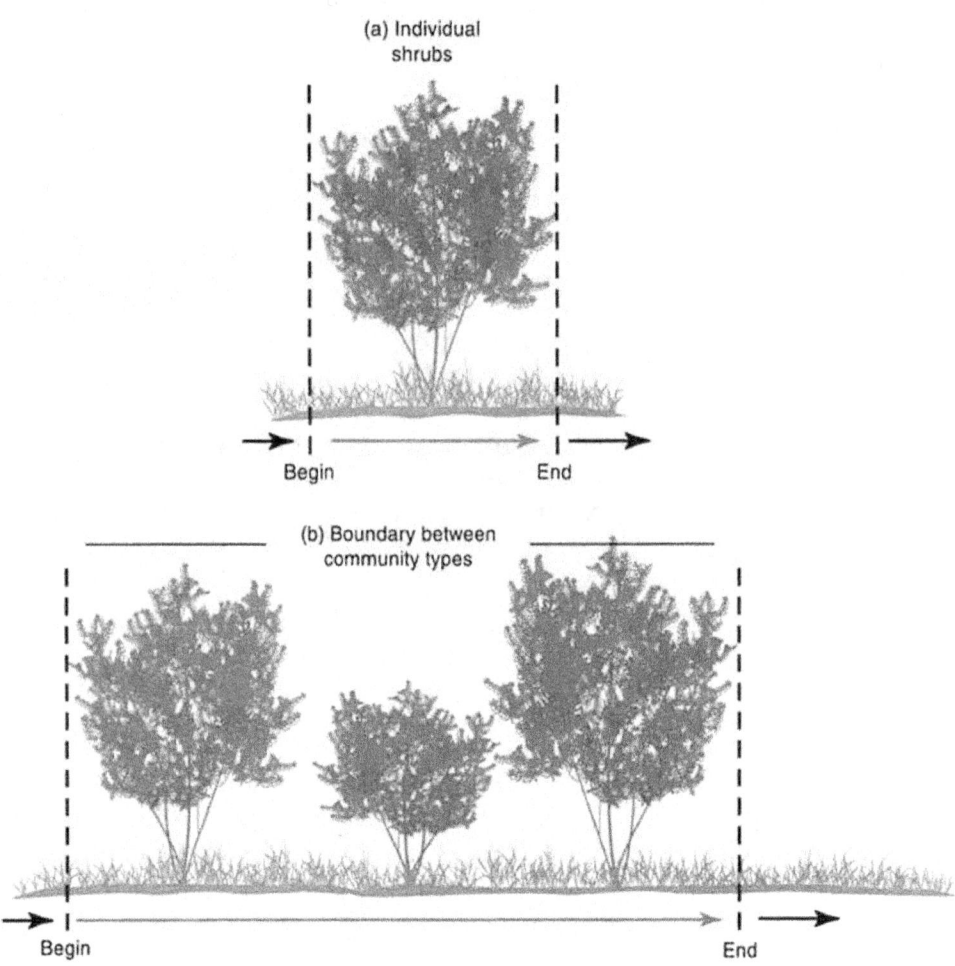

(a) Individual
shrubs

Begin

End

(b) Boundary between
community types

Begin

End

4. When pacing the cross-section or greenline transects, begin and end recording of the shrub and tree overstory at the crown drip line:

Summary

Riparian areas represent the circulatory system of our lands. When the vegetation, water, and soils in these areas are in balance with the climate and landform features, the stream, in turn, maintains a balance with what it gives and takes as it runs over and through the land (figs. 20-23).

This document provides information on three sampling methods used to inventory and monitor the vegetation resources in riparian areas. The vegetation cross-section method is designed to evaluate the health of vegetation across the valley floor. The greenline method is designed to provide a measurement of the streamside vegetation. The woody species regeneration method is designed to measure the density and age class structure of any shrub or tree species that may be present in the sampling area. Together these three sampling procedures can provide an evaluation of the health of all the vegetation in a given riparian area.

30

USDA Forest Service Gen. Tech. Rep. RMRS-GTR-47. 2000

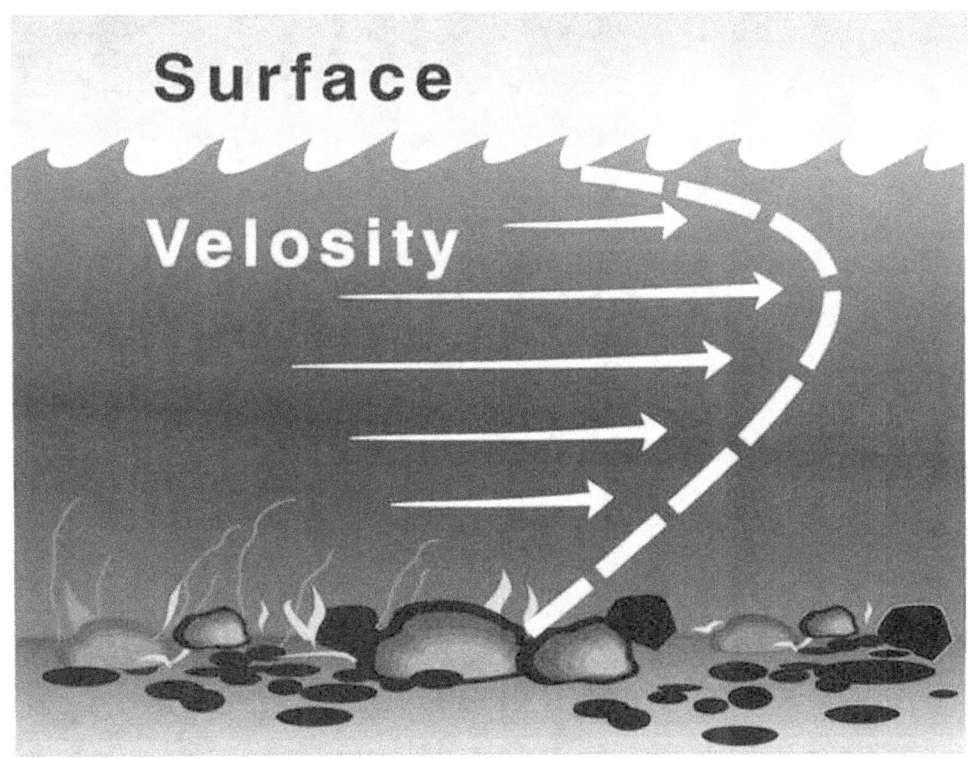

Figure 20—Location of greatest water velocity in a stream (side view).

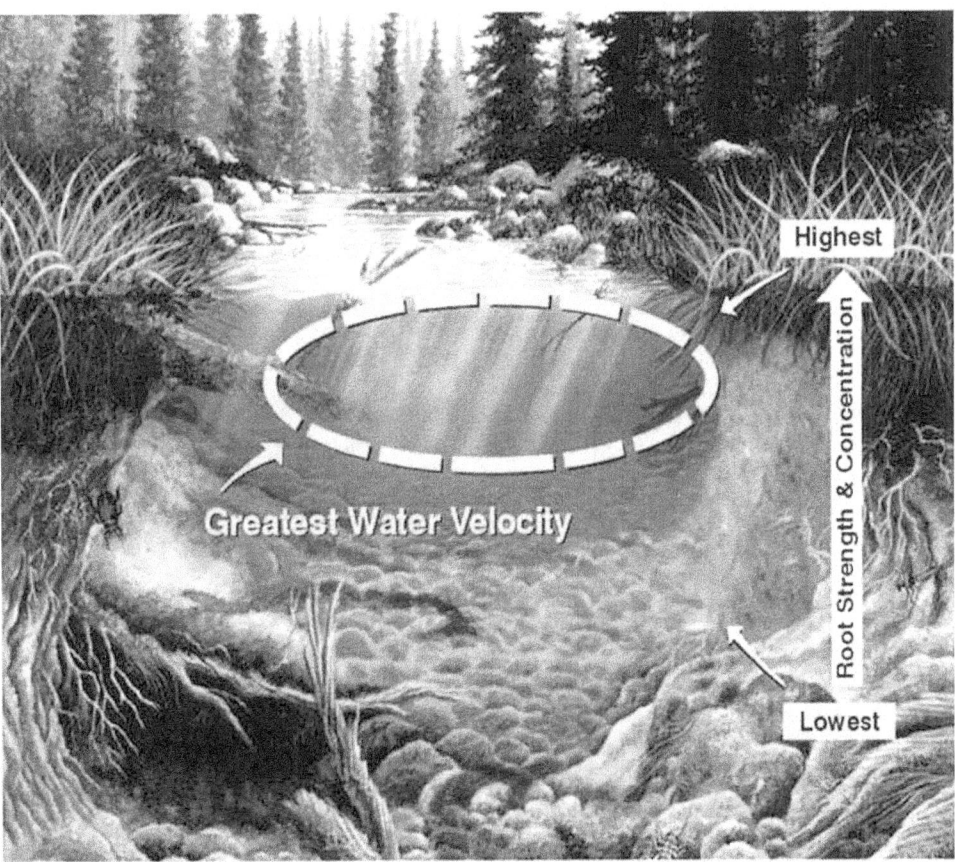

Figure 21—Location of greatest water velocity in a stream in relation to the highest root strength and concentration in the streambank (front view).

USDA Forest Service Gen. Tech. Rep. RMRS-GTR-47. 2000

31

Figure 22 — The combination of greatest water velocity and highest rooting strength and concentration in healthy riparian systems creates undercut banks, which in turn provide a cooling effect in the water column as well as other special habitat features beneficial to many aquatic organisms.

Figure 23 — Example of a healthy riparian area: Cross-Section = PNC; Greenline = PNC; Woody Regeneration = Healthy; and Bank Stability = Excellent.

References

Cagney, Jim. 1993. Riparian management—greenline riparian-wetland monitoring. TR 1737-8. Denver, CO: U.S. Department of the Interior, Bureau of Land Management, Service Center. 45 p.

Cainfield, R. H. 1941. Application of the line interception method in sampling range vegetation. Journal of Forestry. 39: 388-394.

Dunaway, D.; Swanson, S. R.; Wendel, J.; and Clary, W. 1994. The effect of herbaceous plant communities and soil texture on particle erosion of alluvial streambanks. Geomorphology. 9: 47-56.

Hall, Frederick C. 1999. Test of observer variability in measuring riparian shrub twig length. Journal of Range Management. 52 (6): 633-636.

Kleinfelder, D.; Swanson, S.; Norris, G.; Clary, W. 1992. Unconfined compressive strength of some streambank soils with herbaceous roots. Soil Science Society of America Journal. 56 (6): 1920-1925.

Manning, M. E.; Swanson, S. R.; Svejcar, T. J.; Trent, J. 1989. Rooting characteristics of four intermountain meadow communities. Journal of Range Management. 42 (4): 309-312.

Manning, Mary E.; Padgett, Wayne G. 1995. Riparian community type classification for Humboldt and Toiyabe National Forests, Nevada and Eastern California. R4-Ecol-95-01. Ogden, UT: U.S. Department of Agriculture, Forest Service, Intermountain Region. 306 p.

Maxwell, James R.; Edwards, J.; Jensen, Mark E.; Paustian, Steven J.; Parrot, Harry; Hill, Donley M. 1995. A hierarchical framework of aquatic ecological units in North America (Nearctic Zone). Gen. Tech. Rep. NC-176. St. Paul, MN: U.S. Department of Agriculture, Forest Service, North Central Forest Experiment Station. 72 p.

Padget, W. G.; Youngblood, A. P.; Winward, A. H. 1989. Riparian community type classification of Utah and southeastern Idaho. R4-Ecol-89-01. Ogden, UT: U.S. Department of Agriculture, Forest Service, Intermountain Region. 191 p.

Rosgen, David L. 1996. Applied river morphology. Pagosa Springs, CO: Wildland Hydrology. Paginated by Chapter.

U.S. Department of Agriculture, Forest Service. 1992. Integrated riparian evaluation guide. Ogden, UT: U.S. Department of Agriculture, Forest Service, Intermountain Region, 60 p.

U.S. Department of Agriculture. 1993. F.S. 2209.21-Rangeland ecosystem analysis and management handbook. Region 4 Amendment NO. 2209-21-93-1. Ogden, UT: U.S. Department of Agriculture, Forest Service, 20 p.

U.S. Department of Interior. 1998. Riparian area management-process for assessing proper functioning condition. Tech. Reference 1737-9. Denver, CO: U.S. Department of the Interior, Bureau of Land Management. 51 p.

Weixelman, Dave A.; Zamadio, Desierio C.; Zamudio, Karen A. 1996. Central Nevada riparian field guide. R4-Ecol-96-01. Odgen, UT: U.S. Department of Agriculture, Forest Service, Intermountain Region. Variously paged.

Winward, A. H. 1989. Calculating ecological status and resource value rating in riparian areas. In: Clary, Warren P.; Webster, Bert F. 1989. Managing grazing of riparian areas in the Intermountain Region. Gen. Tech. Rept. INT 263. Ogden, UT: U.S. Department of Agriculture, Forest Service, Intermountain Research Station. 11 p.

Winward, Alma H. 1986. Vegetation characteristics of riparian areas. In: Transactions of the Western Section of the Wildlife Society. Sparks, NV: Wildlife Society: 98-101.

Winward, A. H.; Padgett, W. G. 1989. Special considerations when classifying riparian areas. In: Land classifications based on vegetation: applications for resource management. Gen. Tech. Rept. INT-257. Moscow, ID: U.S. Department of Agriculture, Forest Service, Intermountain Research Station. 176-179.

Youngblood, A. P.; Padgett, W. G.; Winward, A. H. 1985. Riparian community type classification of eastern Idaho-western Wyoming. R4-Ecol-85-01. Ogden, UT: U.S. Department of Agriculture, Forest Service, Intermountain Region. 78 p.

USDA Forest Service Gen. Tech. Rep. RMRS-GTR-47. 2000

33

Appendix A: Key to Greenline Riparian Capability Groups _____

Percent gradient and substrate classes modified from Rosgen (1996).

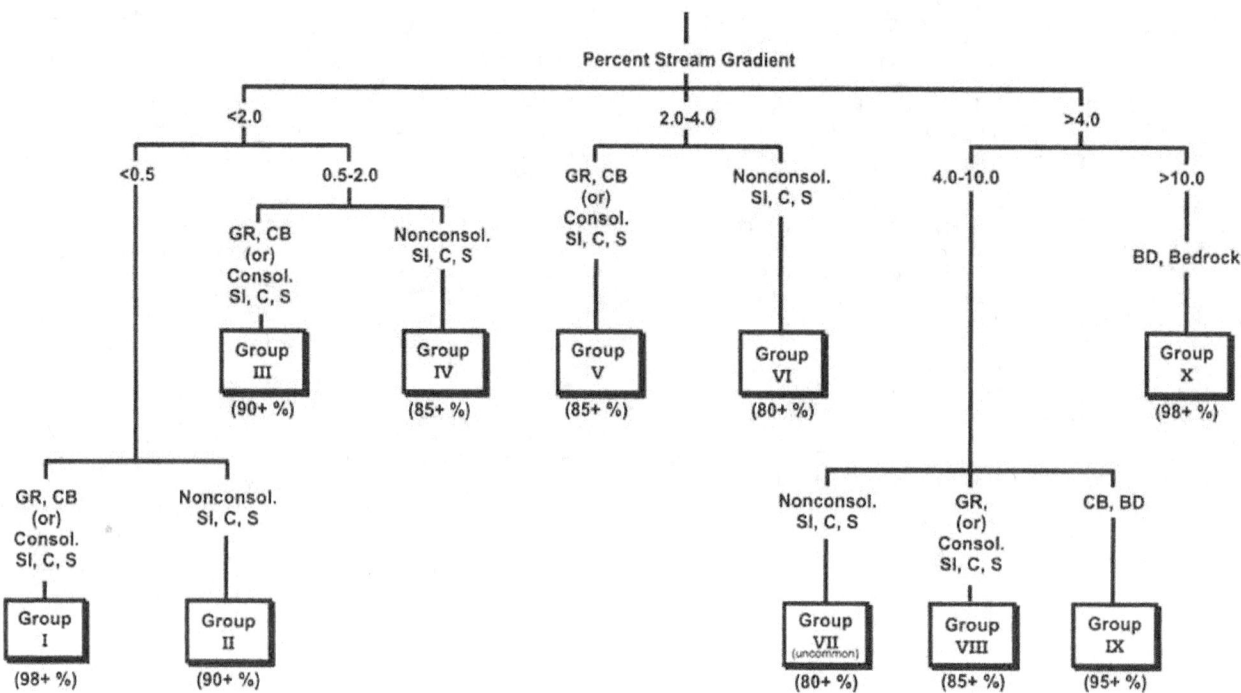

Abreviations Used:

SI	Silt	<0.062mm
C	Clay	<0.062 mm
S	Sand	0.062-2.0 mm
GR	Gravel	0.08-2.5 in
CB	Cobble	2.5-10 in
BD	Boulder	>10 in
Consol	Consolidated Material	
Non-Consol	Non-Consolidated Material	

(Consolidated material refers to situations where at least one major soil horizon within the rooting zone consists of strongly compacted, cohesive, or cemented particles.)

Values in parentheses refer to percent of the greenline that should be represen ed by late seral community types or anchored rocks/logs when riparian areas fitting each capability group are functioning properly.

34

USDA Forest Service Gen. Tech. Rep. RMRS-GTR-47. 2000

Appendix B: Riparian Community Types of the Intermountain Region, Forest Service

The following list of community types represents a summary of types taken from Youngblood and others (1985), Padgett and others (1989), and Manning and Padgett (1995). Each community type has been assigned an "L" if it is known to occur in the latter successional stages along the greenline or an "E" if it occurs in earlier stage of succession along the greenline. Additionally, each community type has been assigned a greenline stability class ranking, ranging from 1 (least) to 10 (greatest), rating its ability to buffer the forces of moving water (see footnotes 1-4, page 39). As community type classifications are developed for other areas, successional status categories (early or late) and bank stability ratings (1-10) will need to be developed for each of these types.

Abbreviation	Community type name	Stability class (veg)	Successional status[a] (greenline)
Coniferous tree-dominated community types			
Conif/Acco	Conifer/*Aconitum columbianum* c.t.	6	E
Conif/Acru	Conifer/*Actaea rubra* c.t.	6	E
Conif/Beoc	Conifer/*Betula occidentalis* c.t.	8	L
Conif/Caca	Conifer/*Calamagrostis canadensis* c.t.	8	L
Conif/Cose	Conifer/*Cornus sericea* c.t.	8	L
Conif/Dece	Conifer/*Deschampsia cespitosa* c.t.	5	E
Conif/Elgl	Conifer/*Elymus glaucus* c.t.	6	E
Conif/Eqar	Conifer/*Equisetum arvense* c.t.	7	L
Conif/MF	Conifer/Mesic Forb c.t.	6	E/L[b]
Conif/Pofr	Conifer/*Potentilla fruticosa* c.t.	6	E
Conif/Popr	Conifer/*Poa pratensis* c.t.	5	E
Conif/Rowo	Conifer/*Rosa woodsii* c.t.	7	E
Conif/TF	Conifer/Tall Forb c.t.	6	E
Picea/Caca	*Picea/Calamagrostis canadensis* c.t.	8	L
Picea/Cost	*Picea/Cornus stolonifera* c.t.	8	L
Picea/Begl	*Picea/Betula glandulosa* communities	9	L
Picea/Eqar	*Picea/Equisetum arvense* c.t.	7	L
Picea/Gatr	*Picea/Galium triflorum* c.t.	6	E
Pico/Casc	*Pinus contorta/Carex scopulorum* c.t.	8	L
Tall deciduous tree-dominated community types			
Acne/Cose	*Acer negundo/Cornus sericea* c.t.	9	L
Acne/Eqar	*Acer negundo/Equisetum arvense* c.t.	8	E
Poan/Beoc	*Populus angustifolia/Betula occidentalis* c.t.	8	L
Poan/Cose	*Populus angustifolia/Cornus sericea* c.t.	8	L
Poan/Cost	*Populus angustifolia/Cornus stolonifera* c.t.	8	L
Poan/Popr	*Populus angustifolia/Poa pratensis* c.t.	6	E
Poan/Rhar	*Populus angustifolia/Rhus aromatica* c.t.	6	E
Poan/Rowo	*Populus angustifolia/Rosa woodsii* c.t.	7	E
Popul/Bar	*Populus*/Bar c.t.	6	E
Popul/Beoc	*Populus/Betula occidentalis* c.t.	8	L
Popul/Cose	*Populus/Cornus sericea* c.t.	8	L
Popul/Rhar	*Populus/Rhus aromatica* c.t.	6	E
Popul/Rowo	*Populus/Rosa woodsii* c.t.	7	E
Popul/Salix	*Populus/Salix* c.t.	8	L
Potr/Beoc	*Populus tremuloides/Betula occidentalis* c.t.	8	L

(con.)

Abbreviation	Community type name	Stability class (veg)	Successional status[a] (greenline)
Potr/Cose	*Populus tremuloides/Cornus sericea* c.t.	8	L
Potr/DG	*Populus tremuloides/Dry Graminoid* c.t.	6	E
Potr/MF	*Populus tremuloides/Mesic Forb* c.t.	6-8	E/L[b]
Potr/Rowo	*Populus tremuloides/Rosa woodsii* c.t.	6	E
Potr/Salix	*Populus tremuloides/Salix* c.t.	8	L

Low deciduous tree-dominated community types

Abbreviation	Community type name	Stability class (veg)	Successional status[a] (greenline)
Alin/Bench	*Alnus incana/Bench* c.t.	6	E
Alin/Cose	*Alnus incana/Cornus sericea* c.t.	8	L
Alin/Eqar	*Alnus incana/Equisetum arvense* c.t.	7	E
Alin/MF	*Alnus incana/Mesic Forb* c.t.	6-8	E/L[b]
Alin/MG	*Alnus incana/Mesic Graminoid* c.t.	6-8	E/L[c]
Alin/Rihu	*Alnus incana/Ribes hudsonium* c.t.	7	L
Beoc/Bench	*Betula occidentalis/Bench* c.t.	6	E
Beoc/Cose	*Betula occidentalis/Cornus sericea* c.t.	8	L
Beoc/Equis	*Betula occidentalis/Equisetum* c.t.	7	E
Beoc/MF	*Betula occidentalis/Mesic Forb* c.t.	6-8	E/L[b]
Beoc/MG	*Betula occidentalis/Mesic Graminoid* c.t.	6-8	E/L[c]

Nonwillow shrub-dominated community types

Abbreviation	Community type name	Stability class (veg)	Successional status[a] (greenline)
Arca/Dece	*Artemisia cana/Deschampsia cespitosa* c.t.	4	E
Arca/DG	*Artemisia cana/Dry Graminoid* c.t.	4	E
Arca/Feid	*Artemisia cana/Festuca idahoensis* c.t.	4	E
Arca/Feov	*Artemisia cana/Festuca ovina* c.t.	4	E
Arca/MG	*Artemisia cana/Mesic Graminoid* c.t.	4-6	E/L[c]
Arca/Popr	*Artemisia cana/Poa pratensis* c.t.	4	E
Artrt/Rowo	*Artemisia tridentata /Rosa woodsii* c.t.	5	E
Cose	*Cornus sericea* c.t.	7	L
Cose-Salix	*Cornus sericea-Salix* c.t.	8	L
Cose/Gatr	*Cornus sericea/Heracleum lanatum* c.t.	7	L
Pofr/Dece	*Potentilla fruticosa/Deschampsia cespitosa* c.t.	5	E
Pofr/Feid	*Potentilla fruticosa/Festuca idahoensis* c.t.	5	E
Pofr/Ligr	*Potentilla fruticosa/Ligusticum grayii* c.t.	5	E
Pofr/Popr	*Potentilla fruticosa/Poa pratensis* c.t.	5	E
Prvi/Rowo	*Prunus virginiana/Rosa woodsii* c.t.	6	E
Rhal	*Rhamnus alnifolia* c.t.	8	E
Rowo	*Rosa woodsii* c.t.	6	E

Low willow-dominated community types

Abbreviation	Community type name	Stability class (veg)	Successional status[a] (greenline)
Low Salix/MF	Low Salix/Mesic Forb c.t.	7-9	E/L[b]
Saea	*Salix eastwoodiae* c.t.	8	L
Saea/Casc	*Salix eastwoodiae/Carex scopulorum* c.t.	10	L
Saor/Dece	*Salix orestera/Deschampsia cespitosa* c.t.	8	E
Saor/TF	*Salix orestera/Tall Forb* c.t.	8-9	E
Sapl	*Salix planifolia* c.t.	8	L
Sapl/Caaq	*Salix planifolia/Carex aquatilis* c.t.	10	L
Sapl/Caca	*Salix planifolia/Calamagrostis canadensis* c.t.	10	L
Sapl/Casc	*Salix planifolia/Carex scopulorum* c.t.	10	L
Sapl/Dece	*Salix planifolia/Deschampsia cespitosa* c.t.	8	E
Sawo/Caaq	*Salix wolfii/Carex aquatilis* c.t.	10	L
Sawo/Caut	*Salix wolfii/Carex utriculata* (formerly *C. rostrata*) c.t.	10	L

(con.)

Abbreviation	Community type name	Stability class (veg)	Successional status[a] (greenline)
Sawo/Casc	*Salix wolfii/Carex scopulorum* c.t.	10	L
Sawo/Dece	*Salix wolfii/Deschampsia cespitosa* c.t.	8	E
Sawo/MF	*Salix wolfii/*Mesic Forb c.t.	7-9	E/L[b]

Tall willow-dominated community types

Abbreviation	Community type name	Stability class (veg)	Successional status[a] (greenline)
Sabe/MG	*Salix bebbiana/*Mesic Graminoid c.t.	7-10	E/L[c]
Sabo/Caaq	*Salix boothii/Carex aquatilis* c.t.	10	L
Sabo/Caca	*Salix boothii/Calamagrostis canadensis* c.t.	10	L
Sabo/Cane	*Salix boothii/Carex nebrascensis* c.t.	10	L
Sabo/Caut	*Salix boothii/Carex utriculata* (formerly *C. rostrata*) c.t.	10	L
Sabo/Eqar	*Salix boothii/Equisetum arvense* c.t.	7	E
Sabo/MF	*Salix boothii/*Mesic Forb c.t.	7-8	E/L[b]
Sabo/MG	*Salix boothii/*Mesic Graminoid c.t.	7-10	E/L[c]
Sabo/Popa	*Salix boothii/Poa palustris* c.t.	7	E
Sabo/Popr	*Salix boothii/Poa pratensis* c.t.	7	E
Sabo/Smst	*Salix boothii/Smilacina stellata* c.t.	7	L
Sadr	*Salix drummondiana* c.t.	7	L
Saex/Barren	*Salix exigua/*Barren c.t.	6	E
Saex/Bench	*Salix exigua/*Bench c.t.	5	E
Saex/Eqar	*Salix exigua/Equisetum arvense* c.t.	7	E
Saex/MF	*Salix exigua/*Mesic Forb c.t.	7-8	E/L[b]
Saex/MG	*Salix exigua/*Mesic Graminoid c.t.	7-10	E/L[c]
Saex/Popr	*Salix exigua/Poa pratensis* c.t.	6	E
Saex/Rowo	*Salix exigua/Rosa woodsii* c.t.	8	E
Sage/Caaq	*Salix geyeriana/Carex aquatilis* c.t.	10	L
Sage/Caca	*Salix geyeriana/Calamagrostis canadensis* c.t.	9	L
Sage/Caut	*Salix geyeriana/Carex utriculata* (formerly *C. rostrata*) c.t.	10	L
Sage/Dece	*Salix geyeriana/Deschampsia cespitosa* c.t.	7	E
Sage/MF	*Salix geyeriana/*Mesic Forb c.t.	7-8	E/L[b]
Sage/MG	*Salix geyeriana/*Mesic Graminoid c.t.	7-10	E/L[c]
Sage/Popa	*Salix geyeriana/Poa palustris* c.t.	6	E
Sage/Popr	*Salix geyeriana/Poa pratensis* c.t.	6	E
Sala1/Bench	*Salix lasiandra/*Bench c.t.	6	E
Sala1/MF	*Salix lasiandra/*Mesic Forb c.t.	7-8	E/L[b]
Sale/Bench	*Salix lemmonii/*Bench c.t.	6	E
Sale/Casc	*Salix lemmonii/Carex scopulorum* c.t.	10	L
Sale/Caaq	*Salix lemmonii/Carex aquatilis* c.t.	10	L
Sale/MF	*Salix lemmonii/*Mesic Forb c.t.	7-8	E/L[b]
Sale/MG	*Salix lemmonii/*Mesic Graminoid c.t.	7-10	E/L[c]
Sale/Seep	*Salix lemmonii/*Seep c.t.	7	L
Sale/TF	*Salix lemmonii/*Tall Forb c.t.	7	E
Sala2/Barren	*Salix lasiolepis/*Barren c.t.	6	E
Sala2/Bench	*Salix lasiolepis/*Bench c.t.	6	E
Sala2/Rowo	*Salix lasiolepis/Rosa woodsii* c.t.	7	E
Salu	*Salix lutea* c.t.	6	L
Salu/Bench	*Salix lutea/*Bench c.t.	6	e
Salu/MF	*Salix lutea/*Mesic Forb c.t.	6-10	E/L[b]
Salu/MG	*Salix lutea/*Mesic Graminoid c.t.	6-10	E/L[c]
Salu/Popr	*Salix lutea/Poa pratensis* c.t.	6	E
Salix/Rowo	*Salix/Rosa woodsii* c.t.	8	E
Salix/Caut	*Salix/Carex utriculata* (formerly *C. rostrata*) c.t.	10	L

(con.)

USDA Forest Service Gen. Tech. Rep. RMRS-GTR-47. 2000

37

Abbreviation	Community type name	Stability class (veg)	Successional status[a] (greenline)
Salix/MF	*Salix*/Mesic Forb c.t.	6-8	E/L[b]
Salix/MG	*Salix*/Mesic Graminoid c.t.	6-10	E/L[c]
Salix/Popr	*Salix*/*Poa pratensis* c.t.	6	E
Salix/TF	*Salix*/Tall Forb c.t.	7	E

Forb-dominated community types

Abbreviation	Community type name	Stability class (veg)	Successional status[a] (greenline)
Anki	*Angelica kingii* c.t.	5	E
Asch	*Aster chilensis* c.t.	4	E
Asin-Dain	*Aster integrifolius-Danthonia intermedia* c.t.	3	E
Asin-Dece	*Aster integrifolius-Deschampsia cespitosa* c.t.	3	E
Asin-Feid	*Aster integrifolius-Festuca idahoensis* c.t.	3	E
Cale	*Caltha leptosepala* c.t.	6	E
Carda	*Cardamine* spp. c.t.	4	E/L[d]
Ciar	*Cirsium arvense* c.t.	6	E
Doje	*Dodecatheon jeffreyi* c.t.	3	E
Eqar	*Equisetum arvense* c.t.	5	E
Equis	*Equisetum* spp. c.t.	7	L
Irmi/DG	*Iris missouriensis*/Dry Graminoid c.t.	6	E
Irmi/MG	*Iris missouriensis*/Mesic Graminoid c.t.	6-8	E
Lupo-Setr	*Lupinus polyphyllus-Senecio triangularis* c.t.	5	E
Mear	*Mentha arvensis* c.t.	4	E/L[d]
Meci	*Mertensia ciliata* c.t.	7	L
MFM	Mesic Forb Meadow c.t.	4-6	E/L[b]
Migu	*Mimulus guttatus* c.t.	3	E/L[d]
Naof	*Nasturtium officinale* [*Rorippa nasturtium-aquaticum*] c.t.	4	E/L[d]
Raaq	*Ranunculus aquatilis* c.t.	4	E/L[d]
Soca	*Solidago canadensis* c.t.	8	L
Tyla	*Typha latifolia* c.t.	9	L
Urdi	*Urtica dioica* c.t.	7	E
Veam	*Veronica americana*	3	E/L[d]
Veca	*Veratrum californicum* c.t.	6	E

Graminoid-dominated community types

Abbreviation	Community type name	Stability class (veg)	Successional status[a] (greenline)
Alar	*Alopecurus arundinaceus* c.t.	6	E
Agsc	*Agrostis scabra* c.t.	2	E
Agst	*Agrostis stolonifera* c.t.	3	E
Alaq	*Alopecurus aequalis* c.t.	3	E/L[d]
Alge	*Alopecurus geniculatus* c.t.	3	E/L[d]
Caca	*Calamagrostis canadensis* c.t.	8	L
Cane2	*Calamagrostis neglecta* [*C. stricta*] c.t.	7	L
Caaq	*Carex aquatilis* c.t.	9	L
Caaq2	*Catabrosia aquatica* c.t.	3	E/L[d]
Cabu	*Carex buxbaumii* c.t.	8	L
Cado	*Carex douglasii* c.t.	4	E
Cala1	*Carex lasiocarpa* c.t.	9	L
Cala2	*Carex lanuginosa* c.t.	9	L
Cale	*Carex lenticularis*	4	E
Cali	*Carex limosa* c.t.	8	L
Cami	*Carex microptera* c.t.	4	E
Cane	*Carex nebrascensis* c.t.	9	L
Caut	*Carex utriculata* (formerly *C. rostrata*) c.t.	9	L

(con.)

Abbreviation	Community type name	Stability class (veg)	Successional status[a] (greenline)
Casa	*Carex saxatilis* c.t.	8	L
Casc	*Carex scopulorum* c.t.	9	L
Casi	*Carex simulata* c.t.	8	E/L
Dain	*Danthonia intermedia* c.t.	3	E
Dece	*Deschampsia cespitosa* c.t.	4	E
Dece-Cane	*Deschampsia cespitosa-Carex nebrascensis* c.t.	7	L
Elpa1	*Eleocharis palustris* c.t.	6	E
Elpa2	*Eleocharis pauciflora* c.t.	5	E
Glyce	*Glyceria* spp. c.t.	8	E/L
Hobr	*Hordeum brachyantherum* c.t.	3	E
Hoju	*Hordeum jubatum* c.t.	2	E
Juba	*Juncus balticus* c.t.	9	L
Juen	*Juncus ensifolius* c.t.	7	L
Muan	*Muhlenbergia andina* c.t.	3	E
Muri	*Muhlenbergia richardsonis* c.t.	3	E
Phar	*Phalaris arundinacea* c.t.	9	L
Phma (Phau)	*Pragmites communis* (*P. australis*) c.t.	9	L
Pone	*Poa nevadensis* c.t.	3	E
Popr	*Poa pratensis* c.t.	3	E
Scac	*Scirpus acutus* c.t.	9	L
Scmi	*Scirpus microcarpus* c.t.	9	L
Scpu	*Scirpus pungens* c.t.	7	E
Nonvegetated types			
Barren	Barren	1	E
Rock	Anchored Rock	10	L
Log	Anchored Log	10	L

[a]The successional status ratings (E and L) and the vegetation stability class ratings (1-10) used in this appendix were developed based on several years of observations and study of various successional sequences as well as in-field evidence of their abilities to withstand the erosive forces of water. Information from various research studies also was used where it was available. A few values have been adjusted slightly in this document as continuing field experiences and recommendations from other riparian ecologists have demonstrated a need for such modifications.

[b]These types are considered late seral only if the following, or similar, mesic/hydrophtic forbs dominate the undergrowth (at least 20 percent cover):

Angelica kingii	*Mertensia ciliata*
Equisetum spp.	*Saxifraga odontoloma*
Urtica dioica	

[c]These types are considered late seral only if the following, or similar, mesic/hydrophytic graminoids dominate the undergrowth (at least 25 percent cover):

Carex lanuginosa	*Carex nebrascensis*
Juncus balticus	

[d]These types are dominated by early colonizing species and are considered late seral only when they occur in settings where the adjacent community types (those dominated by stabilizing species that serve as backup protection on the same stream footage) are rated Late. For example, 5 steps of *Catabrosia aquatica* backed up by *Carex nebrascensis* = L while 5 steps of *Catabrosia aquatica* backed by *Agrostis stolonifera* = E.

Appendix C: Examples of Greenline Ecological Status and Stability Rating

Example: Greenline Ecological Status

Area: Willow Creek, Strawberry Valley,
7,000 feet, 2.5% gradient, non-consolidated cobble/gravel

Greenline	Composition	Ecological status (Early)	(Late)
Popr	70	70	
Caut	10		10
Sabo/Popr	03	03	
Sabo/MF	02		02
Raaq	05	05	
Caaq	05	05	
Rock	02		02
Agst	03	03	
Total	100%	86	14

Ecological Status

$$0–15 = \text{Very Early}$$
$$16–40 = \text{Early} \longleftrightarrow {}^{14}/_{85*} = 16 \% = \text{Early}$$
$$41–60 = \text{Mid}$$
$$61–85 = \text{Late}$$
$$86+ = \text{PNC}$$

*From Capability Group (Appendix A, page 34)

Example: Greenline Stability Rating

Greenline	Composition	Stability (Class)	(Index)
Popr	70	3	2.10
Caut	10	9	.90
Sabo/Popr	03	6	.18
Sabo/MF	02	6	.12
Raaq	05	4	.20
Caaq	05	3	.15
Rock	02	9	.18
Agst	03	3	.09
Total	100%		3.92

Stability Rating

$$0–2 = \text{Very Poor (very low)}$$
$$3–4 = \text{Poor (low)} \longleftrightarrow 3.92 = \text{Poor (low)}$$
$$5–6 = \text{Moderate}$$
$$7–8 = \text{Good (high)}$$
$$9–10 = \text{Excellent (very high)}$$

USDA Forest Service Gen. Tech. Rep. RMRS-GTR-47. 2000

Appendix D: Equipment List _____

Steel fence posts or rebar for permanently marking study locations.

Hammer or post pounder.

Clip board and forms.

Tally counter.

Camera and film.

Plant identification book, and if available, community type book.

Two 3-foot rods for temporarily marking the beginning and ending points of transects.

One 6-foot pole for use in sampling woody species regeneration.

Flagging.

Global positioning system unit (if available).

Appendix E: Forms _____

1—Cross Section Composition (Transect Data)

2—Cross Section Summary Sheet

3—Riparian Greenline Transect Data

4—Greenline Summary Sheet

5—Woody Species Regeneration

6—Woody Species Regeneration Summary

7—Greenline Successional Status Worksheet

8—Greenline Stability Rating (CT's) Worksheet

USDA Forest Service Gen. Tech. Rep. RMRS-GTR-47. 2000

41

CROSS SECTION COMPOSITION
(Transect Data)

Forest / District _____ / _____ Date _____

Drainage _____

Examiners _____ Photo Nos _____

Complex _____

Location _____

Transect No _____   Feet/Step _____

Community Type	NUMBER STEPS													TOTAL STEPS	FEET Optional

ESTIMATED AVERAGE HT.	Sprout	Young	Mature	Decadent	Dead

LINE INTERCEPT CANOPY OF WOODY SPECIES (optional) _____

TOTAL FEET OF RIPARIAN (optional) _____

USDA Forest Service Gen. Tech. Rep. RMRS-GTR-47. 2000

CROSS SECTION SUMMARY SHEET

Forest/District_____/_____ Date Compiled _____

Drainage _____

Examiners _____

Complex _____

Transect No.☞ _____

Community Type	T$_1$ Steps	T$_2$ Steps	T$_3$ Steps	T$_4$ Steps	T$_5$ Steps	TOTAL	PCT COMPOSITION
Total							

	Grand Total	100

TOTAL UNDISTURBED TYPES (PERCENT) _____

Total Steps ea. CT.
---------------------- = Composition
Grand Total Steps

Status (check)

_____ 0 ..15 = very early seral
_____ 16 ..40 = early seral
_____ 41 ..60 = mid seral
_____ 61 ..85 = late seral
_____ 85 + = PNC

RIPARIAN GREENLINE TRANSECT DATA

Forest / District _____ / _____ Date _____

Drainage _____

Examiners _____ Photo Nos _____

Complex _____

Location _____

Transect No. _____ Feet/Step _____

Community Type	STEPS (Left)								STEPS (Right)								TOTAL STEPS	% COMP.

Grand Total

BARS WITHIN TRANSECT (Optional)

	STEPS	FEET
GRAVEL		
SAND		
SILT / CLAY		

Total Steps ea. CT
------------------------- = Composition
Grand Total

GREENLINE SUMMARY SHEET
(Use when more than one greenline measurement is taken within one complex)

Forest / District _____ / _____ Date Compiled _____

Drainage _____

Examiners _____ Photo Nos _____

Complex _____

Transect Nos _____

Community Type	T₁ (Steps) Left	Right	T₂ (Steps) Left	Right	T₃ (Steps) Left	Right	Total Steps	Comp. %

Grand Total

BARS WITHIN ALL TRANSECT (Optional)

	FEET
GRAVEL	
SAND	
SILT / CLAY	

$$\frac{\text{Total Steps ea. C.T.}}{\text{Grand Total}} = \text{Composition}$$

WOODY SPECIES REGENERATION

Forest / District _____ / _____ Date _____

Drainage _____

Examiners _____ Photo No _____

Complex _____

Location _____

Transect No. _____

Species	Seedling / Sprout		Young / Sapling		Mature		Decadent		Dead	
	Left	Right	Left	Right	Left	Right	Left	Right	Left	Right
Total										
Total (L&R)										

Use dot count method to record numbers eg.

$\vdots$ = 4 $\vdots\vdots$ = 8 $\boxtimes$ = 10

Average Height (Optional)

Tree Layer	
Shrub Layer	
Herb Layer	

46

USDA Forest Service Gen. Tech. Rep. RMRS-GTR-47. 2000

WOODY SPECIES REGENERATION SUMMARY

Forest / District _____ / _____ Date _____

Drainage _____ Photo No⬚ _____

Examiners _____

Complex _____

Transect No⬚ _____

Species	Seedling/Sprout			Young/Sapling			Mature			Decadent			Dead		
	T_1	T_2	T_3	T_1	T_2	T_3	T_1	T_2	T_3	T_1	T_2	T_3	T_1	T_2	T_3
TOTAL (ea trans)															
TOTAL (combined)															

Statement of Health and General Comments:

_____
_____
_____
_____
_____
_____
_____

Average Height: (Optional)

Tree Layer	
Shrub Layer	
Herb Layer	

GREENLINE SUCCESSIONAL STATUS WORKSHEET

Complex name: _____

(Stream, Lake, etc; Dominant C.T., Soil Family, Stream Type)

General Location: _____

Community Type	% Composition	SUCCESSIONAL RATING	
		Early	Late
Total	**100%**		

Percent Late Seral Types = _____   Potential (see capability group value) = _____

Successional Status)
(Check One)

_____	0 ...15 =	very early seral
_____	16 ..40 =	early seral
_____	41 ..60 =	mid seral
_____	61 ..85 =	late seral
_____	85 + =	PNC

USDA Forest Service Gen. Tech. Rep. RMRS-GTR-47. 2000

GREENLINE STABILITY RATING (CT's) WORKSHEET

Complex name:

_____

(Stream, Lake, etc; Dominant C.T., Soil Family, Stream Type)

General Area:

_____

Community Type	Composition %	STABILITY	
		Class	Index
Totals	**100%**		

Stability Rating	
_____	0 .. 2 = very poor (very low)
_____	3 .. 4 = poor (low)
_____	5 .. 6 = moderate
_____	7 .. 8 = good (high)
_____	9 .. 10 = excellent (very high)

You may order additional copies of this publication by sending your mailing information in label form through one of the following media. Please specify the publication title and General Technical Report number.

USDA Forest Service
Rocky Mountain Research Station

Telephone	(970) 498-1392
FAX	(970) 498-1396
E-mail	rschneider/@fs.fed.us
Web site	http://www.fs.fed.us/rm
Mailing Address	Publications Distribution
	Rocky Mountain Research Station
	240 West Prospect Road
	Fort Collins, CO 80526

Or

Department of the Interior
Bureau of Land Management

Telephone	(303) 236-0162
FAX	(303) 236-3508
E-mail	dprichard@blm.gov
Mailing Address	Bureau of Land Management
	NARCS, RS-130
	P.O. Box 25047
	Denver, CO 80225-0047

RMRS
ROCKY MOUNTAIN RESEARCH STATION

The Rocky Mountain Research Station develops scientific information and technology to improve management, protection, and use of the forests and rangelands. Research is designed to meet the needs of National Forest managers, Federal and State agencies, public and private organizations, academic institutions, industry, and individuals.

Studies accelerate solutions to problems involving ecosystems, range, forests, water, recreation, fire, resource inventory, land reclamation, community sustainability, forest engineering technology, multiple use economics, wildlife and fish habitat, and forest insects and diseases. Studies are conducted cooperatively, and applications may be found worldwide.

Research Locations

Flagstaff, Arizona	Reno, Nevada
Fort Collins, Colorado*	Albuquerque, New Mexico
Boise, Idaho	Rapid City, South Dakota
Moscow, Idaho	Logan, Utah
Bozeman, Montana	Ogden, Utah
Missoula, Montana	Provo, Utah
Lincoln, Nebraska	Laramie, Wyoming

*Station Headquarters, Natural Resources Research Center, 2150 Centre Avenue, Building A, Fort Collins, CO 80526